THE THIN GREEN LINE

THE MONEY SECRETS OF THE SUPER WEALTHY

Paul Sullivan

SIMON & SCHUSTER

New York London Toronto Sydney New Delhi

Simon & Schuster
1230 Avenue of the Americas
New York, NY 10020

First Simon & Schuster hardcover edition March 2015

SIMON & SCHUSTER and colophon are registered
trademarks of Simon & Schuster, Inc.

For information about special discounts for bulk purchases,
please contact Simon & Schuster Special Sales at
1-866-506-1949 or business@simonandschuster.com.

The Simon & Schuster Speakers Bureau can bring authors to your live event.
For more information or to book an event, contact the
Simon & Schuster Speakers Bureau at 1-866-248-3049 or
visit our website at www.simonspeakers.com.

Interior design by Ruth Lee-Mui
Jacket design by David Drummond
Jacket photograph: Gates and Drive of a Country Estate © 100 Words/Shutterstock

Manufactured in the United States of America

10 9 8 7 6 5 4 3 2 1

Library of Congress Cataloging-in-Publication Data is available.

ISBN 978-1-4516-8724-8
ISBN 978-1-4516-8726-2 (ebook)

To my girls,
Laura, Virginia, and Phoebe

CONTENTS

LUNCHING WITH WEALTHY PEOPLE

On a crisp spring morning, I sat in an exquisitely refurbished town house a block from New York's Metropolitan Museum of Art. I was listening to four men worth tens of millions of dollars argue over who had the poorest childhood.

With servers laying out a multicourse lunch in an opulent drawing room, the men tried to outhumble each other. Allen Wolpert, a former consultant at Arthur Andersen and then Accenture, boasted that he grew up in the Brighton Beach section of Brooklyn and it was rough. His face had a fleshiness often associated with men who have risen from nothing to great wealth, but his voice still carried the borough's distinctive, nasally accent. "What block?" shouted Tommy Gallagher, who started on Wall Street right out of high school because he could not get into college. When he heard the answer, he nodded: Wolpert was the real deal. Gallagher may have been wealthy, but he was

Brooklyn through and through. He rose to become the vice chairman of CIBC World Markets when it was a high-flying financial firm. He lived on tony East Seventy-Fifth Street in Manhattan and had a beach house in the Hamptons, the summer retreat for Manhattan's wealthiest. But that day he was dressed in a blue T-shirt underneath an old, green oxford. The combination made him look more like a neighborhood bartender or a washed-up boxer than a decamillionaire. Between them sat Steve L., a proprietary trader in Greenwich, Connecticut. He wanted in on this game. "We had no money," he said, shaking his well-groomed head for emphasis. "I mean, no money. Nothing." When pressed by the other men, Steve L. said his father had been a professor in northern Virginia—a euphemism for the University of Virginia. A college campus was never going to be the mean streets of Brooklyn. He was out.

But then the quiet guy sitting next to me piped up. Steven, a short, soft man in his late fifties who would go unnoticed on a city street, said he had grown up in the Bronx, with a cabbie as a father. Not only did they have no money, but if it hadn't been for a lucky break his father got, he wouldn't be here today. "One of his fares got me into Dartmouth," he said. The group was impressed. He had gone from nothing to beyond the others and had the fortune to prove it. Steven told me he had owned residential real estate in East Harlem but had sold his company in March 2007 at the height of the property bubble. The timing of the sale sounded fortuitous to me, but it didn't raise any red flags. People who invested in real estate could grow exceedingly rich just as quickly as they could lose everything. He had gotten lucky on the timing of his sale, perhaps, but surely he had put a lot of effort into his business. That day, he easily won the humble game. What Steven had left out was that he had once been known as one of the worst slumlords in New York City—a distinction that netted him $225 million for his company.

I listened to these men with a sense of bemusement and fascination. They were all in their fifties, but they had been trying to outdo each other like teenagers. They had succeeded in their professions but could not stop competing. I may not have wanted to have dinner or even a drink with any of them, but I admired what they had done: made themselves financially secure for life through their own work. Their success was appealing to me. It was 2011 and the economic recovery in the United States was weak. I had come to believe that the economy was changing, and that the burden of security in life and retirement was going to fall squarely on each of us. I believed that making money was getting harder, and holding on to it harder still.

These four men were members of Tiger 21, an investment group with some two hundred members in the United States and Canada. To join the group, each man needed at least $10 million and a willingness to pay an annual membership fee of $30,000. In return they met one day every month to talk about their investments, though just as often they discussed their feelings in one of the few groups in the world where they would not be judged as ungrateful rich guys. They were all rich guys, grateful or not. As one of them, Leslie Quick III, son of the founder of the Quick & Reilly discount brokerage, told me, "Where can I talk about my problems and other people won't say, 'You've got a lot of money, bitch, bitch, bitch'? I do have a lot of money, but I still have problems. Sure, they're high-class problems, but they're still problems."

I was there with about a dozen members in my role as the Wealth Matters columnist for the *New York Times*. They were going to examine the investment decisions my wife and I had made the way they examined their own choices. I thought this exercise might make an interesting column. While the monthly Tiger 21 sessions featured updates on the world economy, investment tips, speakers, and a nice lunch—a buffalo-mozzarella-and-tomato salad, poached salmon, and sautéed asparagus; a crisp chardonnay served all around—the signature moment was the Portfolio Defense, whereby one member opens up his investments to the brutal scrutiny of the eleven other people in the group. He must tell the truth and then listen while everything is critiqued. It's tough love. They had promised to analyze the financial decisions my wife and I had made just as they did those of each member. By their standards, the investments we had were insignificant and simple. But personally I wanted to know how my wife and I had thought about our financial lives. I was pretty confident. I thought everything would go well.

The choice of art on the walls—photos of Chinese Communist meeting halls in decay—should have been my clue that this analysis was going to be torturous. The members took turns eviscerating our financial planning. I felt like the sole mole on a Whac-A-Mole board: when one old man's arm got tired, he passed the mallet to another and so on and so on. They weren't mocking our investments—these were men who had tens of millions of dollars on up to Quick, whose family had sold Quick & Reilly for $1.6 billion in 1997. They were tearing us apart for simpler things: our expenses, our insurance, our view of the future being like the present but with additional children. They were attacking us for errors that we had made, but that I was sure other people had made as well. Had we saved all we could? Had we indulged in luxuries that we could pay for but couldn't really afford? Had we planned how we were going to pay for our life if something went wrong? Our income was high, but how long could we replace it if one or both of us lost our jobs or if illness ended our careers? *Risk* was the word I heard over and over. Their judgments of the life we had built, with care and foresight, terrified me.

"Your goal does not match your current reality," said Steve L, the trader. "You're not on a trajectory to get to point B from point A. I'm too short for my weight, but you're spending too much money right now."

He thought our plan to make the same amount of money in the future as we were making now—not more—was unrealistic. The businesses we were in—journalism and recruiting—were changing. And even if our incomes stayed steady, we had no idea what additional children would cost, particularly if we planned to send them to private school and save enough to pay for college. Wolpert, a father of two grown children, chimed in with the consultant's long view: "You're living very comfortably, but this kids thing, it's going to rock your financial stability for the next twenty years while you get the kids through college. The comfort that you have today—ten years from now you may feel yourself being stretched unless your income and your wife's income grow to just accommodate."

Gallagher was adamant that we needed to sell our condo in Florida, a luxury, we admitted. "I don't see why you have a second home," he said. "You can't afford it." We had bought it in flush times, thinking it would rise in value as everyone else did. Now that we had a child, we realized we weren't visiting it as often and could use the money elsewhere. I added that we had been trying to sell it for two years, even lowering the price to below what we'd paid for it. Gallagher thought we should lower it by another 15 percent, a price so low that we would have had to pay an additional $20,000 or $30,000 to the bank. "Write the check," he bellowed. "How much does it cost you to manage it? I have a house at the beach and I say it only costs me a hundred thousand dollars to run, but when I put everything in, it's more like two hundred thousand dollars." He was right about the costs. With the mortgage, condo fees, and utilities each month even if we didn't use the place, it carried what economists call "opportunity costs" and what Tiger members labeled "optionality." The money going to a condo was money that could have been saved, spent on real needs, or kept in reserve for when something went wrong.

Some moments at lunch were helpful. We had life insurance, but we needed more, and term insurance is cheap. We didn't have sufficient coverage for disability, which was statistically more likely to happen than one of us dying young. "That disability policy is just as important as that life insurance policy," said Alan Mantell, an attorney with Woody Allen glasses who had made his money in real estate. "It's probably five times more likely that you'll be disabled than you'll die. It's very expensive insurance and you've got to pay the price." This suggestion played into the theme of risk management. But we had forgotten, or underestimated, something else still. By the end, not even the moments of hypocrisy were enough to make me feel better. Steven, the slumlord, thought we didn't give enough to charity, but he had given only 2 percent of his income to charitable groups when he was building his real estate business—or exploiting poor people with no other options, depending on your point of view. We volunteered to train guide-dog puppies for the blind and donated to that organization every year. Now he gave heavily to his synagogue and the Ivy League college that had changed his life—and taken in at least one of his children. These were the types of soul-cleansing groups—church and college—that people who have led rapacious lives hoped would absolve them. Still, even hearing his absurd advice wasn't enough to lighten the mood. I felt that we were, in a word, screwed.

Yet, Michael Sonnenfeldt, the founder of Tiger 21, put the group's comments into a broader context. Sonnenfeldt is tall and broad with a bald head and neat beard. He has a penchant for wearing Japanese kimonos. "My perception is many people who are not wealthy, they think the key to getting rich is making a lot of money," he said. "But look at all the movie stars and athletes who have made endless amounts of money and are dirt-poor. They're making ten, fifteen million dollars a year, and they get to forty-five years old and they're flat broke." Sonnenfeldt, who had several degrees from the Massachusetts Institute of Technology, had made a lot of money twice: first in redeveloping a massive financial center in New Jersey and then building and selling a merchant bank—not to mention his ability to get two hundred otherwise savvy people to pay him $30,000 a year to sit around and talk about their high-class problems. He wanted me to separate what it meant to be rich from what it meant to be wealthy. "What's seen is the money they made, but what's unseen is the choices that they've made," he said. "It's what allows them to continue to be wealthy. It's more about taking a very long view with all the potential negatives that we all fear."

Hearing him say this caused me to pause. Despite their quirks, Tiger 21 members were wealthy—which I defined as having more money than you needed to do all the things you wanted to do. It wasn't a number so much as a psychological feeling: you weren't worried about running out of money because you had more than enough, even if it might be less than someone who was worried about going broke. Wealthy was different from being rich. Rich was a number, and as we saw in the Great Recession, one that did not equate to being financially secure. Wealthy could be a successful corporate attorney; it could also be a teacher who lived on her pension and savings. Rich was the guy in my town who drove the red Mercedes SL500 roadster, lived in a heavily mortgaged eighty-five-hundred-square-foot home, and had about a month to find a job before he—or his second wife—blew through what little savings he had. I would come to think of the distinction between the two as a thin green line, like a stock chart rising in fits and starts over the decades. Above the green line, no matter where on the chart's progression, were people who were wealthy, from pensioners to billionaires. They were living in financial comfort regardless of the balance in their brokerage accounts. Below the line were people, rich or not, who did not have the security of true wealth. They may have had a lot of money in the bank, but their lifestyles were so extravagant that their finances were fragile, at best. They may have been hanging on to the line by their fingertips. They may have been in free fall without knowing how hard their landing was going to be. And, of course, they may have been among the many who were looking up at the line from far down, hoping to one day surmount it.

"The issue is not in any way to diminish the success you're enjoying," Sonnenfeldt continued. "The issue is to look at the implications of choices you've made relative to the success you've had."

He came back to insurance and the lifestyle expenses, and why a bit of sacrifice now would build savings for a better life in the future. But those were specifics. More broadly, it was choices like this that might make us wealthy and not just another couple who thought they were rich until they weren't.

"I had friends who lived next door when we were your age—they were our best friends," he said. "My wife's family owned the building. They were renting. They had twenty-five thousand dollars of net worth at the time, and they spent it all fixing up the apartment. I never forgot it. I said, 'Who spends twenty-five thousand dollars so you can carpet the walls?' I'm not really judging them. It's now thirty years later. They live a very nice life, but they live more frugally than they did then." But he *was* judging them—what that couple had done was extravagant bordering on foolish. If you're going to carpet the walls of your apartment, at least make sure you own it—and sell it before the fad passes.

As the afternoon came to an end, I was dazed. What did it mean to save like these guys? Why had I not thought more about the difference between what we could afford and what we needed? Should I heed advice from a former slumlord? What would we need to save to one day have enough? As a business journalist for two decades, I think a lot about money and how I and everyone else spend it, save it, and give it away. I'd like to think I knew something about the subject. But I left that afternoon stunned and a little depressed. I felt as if I had not challenged what I was doing with my own money and certainly not the way I would challenge someone I interviewed. When I got off the train in Old Greenwich a few hours later, my wife greeted me in our new car—for which we paid cash—and I slumped into the seat as if we had lost everything. We were going to meet the contractors who were set to renovate two bathrooms in our house—cash again—but that felt unnecessary, frivolous, and most of all destructive to our future. I was shocked by how financially ill prepared we were. I thought I had thought wisely about our finances and been conservative in our assumptions. I realized I didn't know what I didn't know. That was the day I began thinking about this book.

I came to writing about money by accident. After graduating from Trinity College, I went into a PhD program at the University of Chicago to study with the greatest Irish historian of his generation. With his training and mentorship, I thought I was going to become a famous historian, though I would focus on transatlantic immigration. Looking back, I cringe. I knew nothing about fame, the academic job market, or the role of historians in America today. A few weeks into the program, I wised up and realized my aspiration would, at best, land me at a small college somewhere I wouldn't want to live after spending my twenties in one library or another. I knew then that I didn't have the love for my subject to pursue it regardless of the outcome. If someone had told me I could return to my alma mater and be a professor there, I would have kept at it. But that would never have happened. By the latter half of the 1990s, historians of the Irish diaspora were not in great demand. So after getting my master's degree, I moved to New York, where most of my friends from college lived.

It was 1996, a flush time in the US job market, and I landed a job at a financial newsletter. Having taken exactly one economics class in college, I knew the difference between a stock and a bond and macro- and microeconomics, but not much else. That I knew nothing about what I'd be covering—real estate investment trusts and commercial-mortgage-backed securities—didn't bother my editors; they figured I could ask questions and write down the answers the way others before me had done. And that was what I did, often calling back annoyed bankers and traders two or three times for simple things that I had forgotten to ask the first time around. I hated what I was doing, which made it the perfect first job.

As for money, I was afraid of what it could do to you. This fear started young. It began in my childhood, which I thought about as I listened to the men of Tiger 21 play the humble game. When it came to beginnings, I, too, could trump the professor's kid. I had started out fine—a father who inherited his father's small-town businesses—but grew up terrified—bankruptcy, divorced parents, rented duplex that was robbed twice (including once by my only friend on the street), lousy neighborhood, and worse public schools. My childhood was framed by concerns about money and by extension safety and opportunity. We were probably poor, but we clung to that last rung of respectability and called ourselves *lower*-middle-class. If you listened to my mother tell the story, it shouldn't have been like this. I was born to a family with money. And if money still flowed freely, we'd have had none of the problems we had then. But I don't remember any of the things I would associate today with wealth. By the time I was two, the house, the one that meant everything to her but could fit inside my current home twice with room to spare, was gone, sold when my father filed for bankruptcy. That part is pretty much in agreement. The rest is murky. My father says he could have made a go of it in the construction, paving, and trucking businesses he owned had my mother been more supportive. My mother, who hasn't talked to me in years, used to say it was my father's fault for not working hard enough. I'm not inclined to side with either of them: I cut off my father for nineteen years, but today he has reappeared as a doting grandfather; and my mother, who I thought would be a wonderful grandmother, goes to extreme lengths to return Christmas cards I send her. I prefer the facts as I remember them.

My memory doesn't start until I was about five or six. We were living in our third apartment since the house was lost. It was a nice apartment in a rent-with-the-option-to-buy town-house community—nice that is for Ludlow, Massachusetts, which is a town you wouldn't have heard of unless you had to go to the bathroom around exit 7 on the Mass Pike. Ludlow's a former mill town struggling to find industries to provide jobs. I don't have good memories about the town or the people, but I may have grown up there in a time that was a lot better than the present. A childhood friend who still lives nearby said Ludlow was now one of the worst towns for heroin addiction in western Massachusetts. (The drug trade in my day—and this was a town where the dealers, not the buyers, lived—was mostly around pot.) We lived most of my childhood at 73 Motyka Street—our fourth apartment after the move. It was new, but new did not mean nice. Only one other duplex was between us and a subsidized-housing complex; I ran as fast as I could past it to and from the school bus stop. But from there, I got to go to the good elementary school—good being relative.

When I was ten, my parents split, and the divorce that followed knocked us down a bit more. I wasn't thinking in economic terms then. I was too embarrassed that my parents were not together. I thought it was the defining moment of my life, and it was for a while. My years from ten until fourteen were bleak: I was on subsidized lunch; my clothes were shabby; and I was a participant in or observer of a bus-stop brawl about once a week. The only kids I knew whose parents were divorced were *really* poor, such as David's mother, who had a live-in boyfriend and a premium cable-television package. (One way I knew we were not at the bottom of the socioeconomic hierarchy was that we had basic cable; all the really poor kids had HBO, Showtime, and Cinemax, a truism I have never quite figured out.) David, my only friend in the neighborhood, robbed us, an event chock-full of upsides: one, he didn't kill us with the knives he laid out on the kitchen counter, and two, by laying out those knives and rifling through my mother's clothes in the basement, he scared the hell out of her and it was the reason we finally moved. I've always been perversely grateful to him. Within weeks, my grandfather gave my mother the down payment on a condo, and at sixteen, I moved into something we owned for the first time since I was two. That condo might as well have been a mansion. It made my mother so happy. I was thrilled to be in the clean, managed environment of a condominium complex in a town twenty minutes from where I grew up. That more cracked asphalt was around us than grass, and that our unit had paper-thin walls and a basement that flooded, didn't matter as much as her owning it.

Life had been getting better for me for a couple of years before the robbery. I had a cousin who had gone to a small private school a couple of towns away, and my grandfather figured I was just as smart and should apply. He was confident that I would get financial aid to go. Fortunately, he was right. My life started to improve: better teachers, classrooms, activities, food. While other kids balked at the dress code—khakis, a navy blazer, and a white or blue shirt with a tie—it thrilled me: there was no way to know who was poor and who wasn't.

Academically, I thrived. I also stopped worrying about money: my classmates at Wilbraham & Monson Academy were all richer than me, but I was able to differentiate myself in the classroom and the swimming pool. From there, I went to Trinity on financial aid and Chicago on a fellowship. My grandfather made up the occasional shortfalls in the funding of my education. A retired postman who owned his nine-hundred-square-foot house, he was from a generation that saved money and spent it only on what was needed. Without my knowing it then, he was the first person I knew who lived above the thin green line.

At twenty-three, I moved to New York City, but unlike most of my friends, I didn't have a backstop: it was forward or nowhere. So I never had the option not to work, even when I didn't like a job. Instead I just tried to be good at what I was doing, and I ended up working my way up as a journalist—newsletters, a wire service, daily and international newspapers, glossy magazines, and finally the *New York Times*. My life was fun. While my salary rose with each new job, I saved and never spent more than I made. As in never, ever. I kept a running tally in my head of my credit-card charges and never had a balance from one month to the next. If an unexpected cost or purchase cropped up, I'd hold off on buying something nonessential, even if that included going out, until the next month. I wasn't cheap. I took great vacations to places I'd never imagined visiting when I was growing up—Mexico, Spain, even Hearst Castle. I dated often, if not successfully. Then in 2004, I met the woman I later married. She was working as a recruiter then and now. While her childhood in Atlanta had been a lot better than mine—dad a dentist, mom a government worker, younger brother, dogs, house in the suburbs, a cabin on a lake—she did not come from money. She appreciated how hard it was to make it. She also had far fewer emotional feelings around saving, spending, and giving money away than I did. She made more than

I did so her means were greater means, but since I got no pleasure in buying things, we never argued about finances. Three years after meeting—and some twenty-five years after my parents divorced—I got married. I was happy, professionally fulfilled, and financially comfortable. We made enough money to afford a nice life, and we were spending within our means—or so we thought.

My meeting with Tiger 21 had left me feeling insecure about financial decisions, for sure. But it had also left me more curious than before about other people's thinking about money. That fall, the Occupy Wall Street protests began. Seeing people set up encampments against really rich people—Tiger 21–type members, I thought—sent me to the IRS website to find out what it took to be a One Percenter. I knew we lived among rich people, but we certainly did not consider ourselves rich. About 50 percent of Americans, rich or poor, think they're middle-class, a number that is remarkably constant, and we were no different. I might have said upper-middle-class, either hopefully or sheepishly depending on the audience. But the data told me otherwise. It said that being in the One Percent by earnings meant you made about $345,000 a year. My wife and I, it turned out, were the One Percent. (To make it into that category by wealth, it took the Tiger 21 minimum of $10 million in savings, which we did not have.) This revelation should have been great news, but it shocked me. When you make more money than 99 percent of America, you can't pretend you're middle-class. You probably can't say you're upper-middle-class after you hit the 95th percentile. Nope, we were the One Percent. The reviled One Percent, to many.

Having grown up poor, I knew better than most middle- and upper-middle-class kids that having more money rather than less was always a great thing. But I didn't feel that I should be the subject of protests. That should have been reserved for some of the parents in my daughter's preschool class, such as the father who bragged to another father about taking a week off to go puma hunting in Argentina—right after mentioning he had a putting green installed on the lawn of his waterfront home. He was the One Percent, or probably the one-tenth of One Percent. Still, that my daughter once went to school with a puma-hunting, putting-green-building hedge-fund manager's son says something about where we live—which is among rich people, some of whom may also be wealthy. I'm okay with that. Living here offers far more advantages than where I grew up. The streets are safer, for one. The houses, while big and expensive to heat, are attractive. In the summer, when the trees fill in, I can't see my neighbors, and since no one mows his or her own lawn, my weekends are quiet. The schools are top-notch. And we all have seven hundred channels of cable television to choose from. The gigantic downside is that this is not how most of the country—or the world—lives. I worry not for my wife or me but for our children. I suspected during my childhood that the world wasn't as grim as Ludlow, Massachusetts, but will they grow up thinking everything is as rosy as Fairfield County?

As the effects of my afternoon with Tiger 21 wore off, what still intrigued me was that in the banter and the conversations with the broader group, I realized that for all their money they were not any more secure in some of their decisions than most people I knew. In many ways, they were less secure, something that perhaps came from seeing many of their equally smart or smarter friends achieve less, or maybe from having failed at other businesses along the way to wealth. They came with questions. I admired that. Instead of being overconfident, a state that could have been brought about by the fortunes they had amassed, they were seeking guidance: they didn't want to get fleeced out of the money they had made, and they didn't want their kids to be screwed up. Why didn't the rest of us think that way? Why did we talk about the hot stock tip we got from a friend the way some of us bragged (or lied) about sex in high school? Why didn't we work through the calculations for what we would need later in life? Why didn't we think about the benefits of education and the dangers of lying to ourselves about our level of security, financial and otherwise? If there was any reassurance, it might be that the members of Tiger 21 seemed to be asking probing questions of themselves and accepting uncomfortable answers. They weren't hiding from what they didn't know. Of course, the flip side of this was that if these men who had amassed tens, if not hundreds, of millions of dollars were asking rudimentary questions about charity and raising their kids—with the best advisers money could buy—was there hope for anyone else?

The unsatisfying answer, I found, is, it depends. Boston College's Center on Wealth and Philanthropy has polled the super-rich on how they feel about money—and nonrich people's thoughts about it. Their work goes to the heart of one of our biggest problems surrounding wealth: like sex, it can make us happy, but it can also mess us up. Money can be painfully difficult to talk about with our friends, probably more so than sex and certainly more so than disease. Even people with a healthy attitude toward money can find it hard to assess when they're rich and when they're wealthy. Paul Schervish, who runs the Center on Wealth and Philanthropy, found a direct correlation between people's feelings about their financial situation and giving. This wasn't a raw number; it was how they looked at what they had. Before the financial crash, individual giving ticked up noticeably when a person's income crossed $300,000. Families making less than $300,000, which is pretty much everyone not in the One Percent, gave away 2.3 percent of their income; families making more gave away 4.4 percent. One inference from this is that those with earnings that place them in the One Percent feel more secure about their wealth. Yet in another piece of research, Schervish asked respondents for a raw number that would give them financial security: the median response was $20 million. Feeling wealthy, in other words, is fluid.

Today the more popular topic to discuss is income inequality, usually spoken of as the gap between the top earners in America, whose incomes and wealth continued to grow after the Great Recession, and everyone else, whose incomes stagnated or declined and who have little wealth, in terms of investments. The topic gets people riled up because it strikes at the core of what it means to be an American: a level playing field where anyone has the chance to rise to greatness on his or her own merit. But what if income inequality is not an aberration but the norm and we are returning to it? What if more responsibility for what we have or don't have is falling on us? Two economists among more liberal thinkers—Emmanuel Saez of the University of California, Berkeley, and Thomas Piketty of the Paris School of Economics—have created a fascinating compendium of income around the world that goes by an unwieldy name, the World Top Incomes Database. In 2010, the top One Percent of earners in America had 17.42 percent of the wealth in the country, which was just about the same percentage they had in 1936. It was down from the 18.42 percent they had on the eve of the Great Depression in 1929, which in turn was slightly higher than what they had in 2007 (18.33 percent), when the Great Recession began. The highest percentage was in 1916, at 18.57 percent. If one looks for a time of income equality, or at least less income in the hands of the One Percent, it would be the 1970s, a decade remembered more for economic stagnation, high gas prices, and lack of political leadership than equality. In contrast, the One Percent in France, where the economists were raised, had 20.65 percent of the wealth in 1916 but only 8.94 percent in 2006, the last year for which they had data.

The conservative take on inequality looks at different metrics to make its case. Kevin Hassett and Aparna Mathur of the American

Enterprise Institute wrote about what they said were two more accurate measures of inequality: the Consumption Expenditure Survey, which measures what households spend, and the Residential Energy Consumption Survey, which tracks how much people run appliances such as dishwashers and washing machines, if they have them. By the first measure, consumption has been stable since the 1980s and lower-income households are better off. They found that the rich also consume less in recessions, which periodically narrows the gap. By the second measure, poorer people are not only running their washing machines with abandon but they own them (even if they used credit cards to buy them).

I found both of these takes to be coming at the key issue of income inequality with ingrained biases. Saez and Piketty have the very French view of rectifying distortions by taxing higher earners—with Piketty going so far as to call for a global wealth tax. This idea, if ever adopted, would simply put more money in the hands of federal and state bureaucracies that have generally been inept at managing their own budgets. It also fails to account for the propensity of the children and grandchildren of the wealthy to spend their family's fortune quite quickly, putting all that money back into the economy. On the other side, Hassett and Mathur are looking at superficial indicators of how poor people consume and wealthy people cut back in bad times: Who cares about someone's washing-machine usage?

I prefer another economist, Ronald M. Schmidt, at the University of Rochester's business school, who took the analysis of inequality in a different direction. He looked at how educational choices impacted earnings. In comments on a Congressional Budget Office report, he argued that incomes began to diverge greatly from 1979 to 1986, and the gap had actually started to close in the years after the Great Recession. He wrote that income inequality had been declining since 2000—the year after the dot-com bubble burst. What was more compelling to me, though, was his exposition of three male workers who made different educational choices but all finished high school in 1980. One stopped at high school, another got a college degree, and the third went on to graduate school. "In 1987, when these three were between the ages of 25 and 34, the average high school graduate earned $22,595, while a college graduate earned $31,631 and a holder of a graduate degree earned $36,667," Schmidt wrote. "But 20 years later, in 2007, the corresponding averages for male full-time workers ages 45 to 54 were $46,667, $88,242, and $120,391." Here was his key point. "Unequal? Yes. But the increase in inequality arose because these individuals made different decisions about their education, not because tax policy favors the rich. In essence, economic inequality is another term for incentives that encourage investment in education—or, for that matter, starting a new business." He went on to argue against raising taxes on the wealthy, but he also made the case for people to realize that the choices they make in life have economic consequences. If you look at data on the One Percent, his point is born out. About a third of them started businesses. The next big chunk were doctors at 16 percent. Financiers were right behind them at 14 percent. Athletes and celebrities, who may have limited education, were 2 percent of the top group. What wasn't clear from the data was where these people had started out in life—were they born with lots of financial and family advantages that put them ahead of their peers or had they worked their way up?

What I wanted to know, though, was, were top earners wealthy or just rich? I believe that being wealthy and rich are as different as loving someone for life and having sex on a date. There wasn't anything simple that cleaved the have-mores from the haves and the have-nots. The thin green line cut through every income level—the teacher with her pension on the right side of the line and the high-earning but overleveraged financier on the wrong side. After my talk with Tiger

21, I wanted to make sure that my family was above the line. But I also wanted to see how other people thought about that line in every aspect of their financial lives, from investing and saving to spending, giving away, and thinking about the money they had.

To do this, I divided the book that came out of these thoughts into five sections. The first looks at how we think about money and wealth and why being honest about our fears and insecurities around the two is the only way we can make rational decisions. The second looks at three ways to save money, which are not how most people think about saving. The third looks at spending, from how not to go broke to how to enjoy money to how best to use it to educate your children. The fourth looks at giving money away, from charity to inheritances. The fifth looks at the science of testing how we think and talk about money under stress, which is when most people are forced to worry about the decisions they have made—or not. The goal of it all, though, is to empower people to make financial choices that will help them feel wealthy, not enable them to act rich.

THINK ABOUT IT

1

THE OVERLOOKED
SIMPLICITY OF BUCKETS

I wasn't sure I had the right house when my cab stopped in front of the address Richard Thaler had sent me. On one side of the street was a series of old bungalows. Thaler's side was much, much nicer, even though he was just minutes from downtown La Jolla, a series of intersections filled with gas stations, fast-food restaurants, and the kind of stores you find when a strip mall is desperate for tenants. I asked the cab to wait and walked to the door. I was still trying to figure out why one of the leading economic thinkers of his generation and a perennial candidate for the Nobel Prize in Economics was hanging out in a suburb of San Diego. He had told me that he liked to spend winters away from the University of Chicago. Chicago winters are cold, so this was a rational choice. But his neighborhood still puzzled me.

As he swung open the gigantic wood door, I realized I had done what he and his fellow behavioral economists said people do all the time: I had formed an opinion based on my existing biases; these biases had led me to make a series of assumptions that proved to be totally wrong. I saw a crummy downtown mishmash of houses and thought this great theorist of how irrational we can be when it comes to financial decisions was himself irrational. Now, with the door open, I saw a beautiful stone floor leading my eyes to a wall of windows and the Pacific Ocean beyond. It was clear why the houses on his side of the street were nicer.

Thaler was gracious if a bit awkward as he invited me in. Next to the large door, he looked like the Wizard of Oz in beach garb. He was shorter than I had expected, as if economists should be a certain height, and had a small belly that stuck out as he walked me back to the windows. He hadn't been sure why I wanted to talk to him, but he agreed to meet me when I told him I was going to be in San Diego. I wanted to hear about the research he had done in the 1970s and early 1980s that established the field of behavioral economics. That field, instead of presuming we think rationally and will act in our best interest (or at least respond correctly to financial incentives, as classical economics holds), assumes that we often do the opposite. In one of his books, *Nudge,* Thaler has fun with this idea, drawing the distinction between Econs, who weigh all the options and make rational, informed decisions, and Humans, who do not. To me his earlier research was the foundation for just about all productive thinking about money and wealth. Understanding his work was necessary to understanding how we act as we earn, spend, save, flaunt, and in some cases lose money. It distinguished the wealthy from the rich and established, for me, the thin green line.

I wanted to talk to him about what he called "mental accounting." One of the best-known examples of this theory is how people find it easier to make financial decisions if they put money into fictitious buckets designated for particular expenses—rent, food, savings, travel—as opposed to thinking about the money they have as one lump sum to be spent. They set goals for particular bits of money. If you are a classically trained economist, this way of arranging your finances is completely irrational: these buckets do not exist, so why pretend to have them when you could simply spend and save based on economic incentives? In theory, this view is correct. In practice it doesn't work. This realization was Thaler's breakthrough: these fictitious money buckets help us organize our financial lives and make better decisions. They help us think better about money or at least to not be overwhelmed by it. They give us a chance to think like a wealthy person, even if we earn far less than what it would take to be considered rich.

"The reality is this is an approach used by poor people—the money in the jars that people still do," Thaler told me over a glass of white wine. "It is interesting that the very same thing can be comforting to a guy with a hundred million dollars."

Before I knew anything about Thaler or his research, I was a shrewd mental accountant. It wasn't because I was an aspiring economic theorist or a copycat Alex P. Keaton. As a teenager, I didn't have enough money to pay for all the things I wanted. While I didn't use cookie jars to physically separate money—it all sat in a passbook-savings account—I did create separate funds in my head for the things I needed and wanted, such as gas, food, rounds of golf, dates. I honed this practice through college, and it continued when I started working full-time after graduate school. I could have looked at my paycheck and assumed that I would spend it perfectly and run out of money on the last day of the month, having bought what I needed and wanted. But I had learned from experience. Without bucketing, I might run out of money on day 28 only to find that there was something I needed on day 30, which would cause me to regret having bought something I didn't need on day 2. But if I put money into mental buckets—for rent, food, gym membership, dates—I could make a plan. It worked pretty well. I stopped running out of money and I became more disciplined about spending and saving.

The process also gave money a physicality it hadn't had for me. I had a well-developed sense of money in terms of scarcity or abundance. But I hadn't thought much about saving, spending, and giving it away. All of this was happening to me when money was still tangible and not something transmitted electronically through credit and debit cards. That's where buckets come in. Anyone who hopes to get on the wealthy side of the thin green line will know where his or her money is and what it will be used for. That person is going to have a goal for the money. On the other side are people for whom money comes in and goes out without any set plan for its use—or worse, with the assumption that the money will always be coming in. That group doesn't think how money should be parceled out into fictitious buckets until it isn't there.

Thaler began thinking about the choices people made around money when he was researching something seemingly unrelated: the price of death. As a graduate student at the University of Rochester, he was trying to calculate how much a person's life was worth, in the same way someone might try to value a used car. He was asking these questions without thinking about any of the fuzzier things humans think about when they think about valuing themselves and others— such as love, compassion, humor, kindness, greed, selfishness, or lethargy. He was looking at life as if a person were a refrigerator with a replacement cost. His way of quantifying the price was to measure how much more someone would ask to be paid to do a risky job, such as being a miner. "I realized people were not behaving how they were supposed to behave," Thaler said. "They weren't behaving like rational economic agents."

He came up with two questions that he put to various people. How much would you pay to eliminate a one-in-a-thousand risk of immediate death, and how much would you have to be paid to accept the same risk? The answers astonished him. They made no sense. The typical answer for how much people would pay to get rid of the risk was about $200, while they would need to be paid $50,000 to accept the risk. This disparity was illogical or, in the parlance of economists, irrational. It was the same risk, just phrased differently. People were tallying up costs and benefits in their head, but their answers differed based on how he asked the question. To them, taking on any risk of death *should* cost more money than getting rid of that risk. This question has many permutations. An easier one to grasp might be, would you rather go to a doctor who had a 90 percent success rate in the operating room or one who had 10 percent of his patients die? The one who killed 10 percent of his patients, of course, since 90 percent of them lived.

Once Thaler grasped the ramifications of our flawed reasoning, he started thinking about how those biases skewed our thinking about money. That's when he came up with bucketing. "Putting labels on these buckets is a charade but a helpful one," Thaler told me. He outlined an example. Someone worth $10 million with $1 million of that in a home might put $3 million in an emergency fund in case something goes wrong. A different person could also ask that her portfolio be invested 10 percent in real estate, 30 percent in cash, and the rest in equities. It's the same allocation. "Just putting a label on that cash as emergency money doesn't make any difference," Thaler said. "But at some level it makes all the difference. It calms them down."

Decades after Thaler first came up with this, advisers are latching onto the idea of bucketing. Largely, it's good for them to tell a client who is complaining that his portfolio just dropped 10 percent that all of that money was in a bucket the client didn't need—say the one for charity or heirs. The other buckets—for living expenses, travel, what have you—are safe. For wealthier people, an adviser can take this a step further. He can put the living expenses in cash, the vacation money in something a little riskier, and the money that won't be needed anytime soon into the riskiest investments. With the least volatile investments in the bucket for short- and medium-term living expenses and the most volatile ones in the bucket that you won't need for a long time, the client should be able to sleep at night. "Whether or not financial planners have ever heard of mental accounting," Thaler said, "they've intuitively figured out this makes people comfortable."

Mental accounting shows that the stories we tell ourselves about money matter. Budgeting makes perfect sense: it ensures that you can pay your bills or afford something before you buy it. But talking about a budget is dreary. It's like a diet. Mental accounting takes a budget and slices and dices it into more digestible pieces, which you can shuffle and reshuffle to make it more palatable. It's a plan more like Richard Simmons's Deal-A-Meal cards, which allow people to count calories as if they were playing a card game, not sitting in math class. Mental accounting certainly violates the basic principle of economics that money is fungible, that it flows like water. But our behavior also violates those same principles. If we were rational, we'd never buy a home we couldn't afford or save too little for college or fail to put away enough for retirement. But we worry about all of these things, and for good reason: if we haven't screwed them up, one of our friends has.

What I admired about Thaler's work was his success in framing the most important questions in a way that, to use his phrase, nudges people toward a desired action. "I've been on this thirty-year quest to try to figure out ways of producing economic models that are actually descriptive of how people behave, and mental accounting is a big part of that," Thaler said. Retirement savings is one of his passions—and a bucket that people don't often fill high enough. According to the Employee Benefit Research Institute (EBRI) retirement-readiness survey, somewhere between 56 and 58 percent of people will have enough money to cover at least basic retirement expenses. The remaining 40-plus percent are projected to run out of money. Saving for retirement can go a long way to putting you on the right side of the thin green line, though it won't keep you there if you don't have restraint on your spending. But it is a good place to begin. While people are not great at saving for retirement in general, they are foolish when it comes to putting money into 401(k) plans. In many cases the company matches their contribution—essentially doubling a percentage of the money they put in—yet people often fail to even sign up for the plan, let alone have enough deducted each pay period to take full advantage of the match. The EBRI said that 61 percent of American workers were eligible for a 401(k) plan, but only 46 percent of them signed up for one. To counter this laziness, Thaler came up with a strategy he calls "save more tomorrow." The plan has three aspects: first, it automatically enrolls employees in a company's 401(k) plan so their choice is to opt out, not in; second, it asks employees if they want to increase their contributions to their 401(k) plan in the future, and if they agree, it increases their contribution whenever they get a raise so they will not miss the increased deduction from their paycheck; and third, it gives limited options for investing money so the majority of employees would have to opt out of a broadly diversified portfolio. The result is to deter the worst behaviors of people who know little about investing and would most likely do all the wrong things with their money. The retirement bucket fills without their thinking about it. People who elected this option, Thaler's work has shown, watched their savings rates nearly quadruple, going from 3.5 percent of their income to 13.6 percent in forty months on the program. The strategy tricks them into doing the prudent thing. It largely takes any consideration about what else they could do with that money out of their control. It's paternalistic to some, but it helps people who opt into the plan have a chance to be on the right side of the thin green line when they retire—and not be shocked and have to alter their lives radically.

Thaler's mind is not confined solely to erudite thoughts. He thinks a lot about wine, which he likes. He said few of his "wino friends"—his term for wine collectors—can calculate just how much their now-rare, now-expensive bottles of wine would cost them to drink. How much, say, would it cost them to drink a bottle of wine that they bought for $50 but is now worth $500?

"Most people say it doesn't cost me anything," Thaler said. "Some people who I cherish even say I actually make money drinking this wine because it only cost me fifty dollars. That's mental accounting."

The correct answer is $500. The reason they get it wrong is they are confused about the difference between sunk costs and opportunity costs. A sunk cost is the money you already paid for something—the $50 for the bottle of wine ten years ago. The opportunity cost is what you give up by doing something now. In the case of drinking the wine, the person is giving up selling it for $500, drinking it, and getting $500 worth of enjoyment now, or holding on to it for a few more years and seeing if it will be worth more. That's the opportunity they're trading by drinking the wine. In all likelihood, some of those collectors who opt to drink their wine would have a difficult time going out and paying $500 for that same bottle and drinking it with dinner, though that is exactly what they are doing when they drink it today. They prefer to think that drinking it is a deal because they paid $50 for it years ago.

Thaler said he had only one friend who was completely rational—

and when it came to wine, this friend infuriated him: "He likes to tell people in the group that he has bottles of wine that he can't afford to drink, and they say, 'What do you mean?' He says I have bottles of wine worth a thousand dollars, and I can sell them. And he does because he's completely rational. It drives people crazy. I say he's just too cheap to open it and share it with me."

I'd say the friend is probably on the right side of the thin green line. He has a sense of value and cost that eludes people who are just rich. And I'm also sure he occasionally opens one of those expensive bottles of wine and enjoys it, knowing he has sold others at a great profit.

I couldn't leave without asking Thaler what he thought makes someone wealthy. He had a fantastic second home that led me to believe he was quite rich and, given his academic background, probably wealthy, too. He wouldn't talk about his own finances, but he offered thoughts on other people: "My definition . . . is having enough money that you don't have to worry about money." By his standard, few people had achieved that goal. "Go to Costco and the lot is filled with BMWs and Lexuses. They're paying themselves minimum wage to get these things so what is the value of their time?" He thought they would be better off paying full price at a local drugstore and using that extra time for something more productive.

Thaler was surely wealthy. Whatever money he had made in academia and from the consulting that top-tier economists such as him do, he had certainly managed in various buckets. That ability, more so than making more than everyone else, is useful as we start to think about the difference between being wealthy and rich along the continuum of the thin green line: the wealthy are managing Thaler's buckets for various obligations, while the rich are scrambling to make sure their one pot does not hit empty before more money comes in to fill it back up.

SAVE IT

2

CHECKING STOCK QUOTES IS HAZARDOUS TO YOUR WEALTH

Jeannie Krieger had some money to invest. It was the second time she had had a windfall from an unfortunate situation, and she was more circumspect this time around. In the 1980s, when her husband died in a plane crash, she managed the insurance benefits to make sure she and their two school-aged kids were taken care of. She figured it out on her own, asking friends when she didn't understand something. She invested conservatively in stocks and bonds and used some of the insurance money to start a fashion company. "I imported reptile-leather goods from South America," she said. The business was guided as much by her interest in fashion as her MBA and background in accounting. Yet years later when her father, a successful surgeon, died, she felt she needed some help investing the inheritance. She wasn't hoping for a big return, but she didn't want to risk losing it either. So she did what many widows might do: she turned to her family. In this case, she asked her son-in-law for help.

Plenty of sons-in-law would be unqualified to offer advice, but hers had started a financial advisory firm that he had sold to GE Capital a few years earlier. Financially, he was set for life and had some free time. She told me, "My questions to him were: 'Did I have enough resources?' I didn't want to run out of my money. If I continued to spend at the level I was spending, what would that project out to? Would I be okay with that plan? He gave me those kind of parameters. I wanted to know the risk. He took into account absolutely everything I spent. Was I on the right track? I wanted verification." Her biggest concern, though, was a universal one: "What could I spend with a normal life span?"

While her concern was common, her ability to listen to the advice she received was not. When she and I spoke, Krieger, then in her late sixties, described her financial position as "moderate, not megawealth." She had provided her son-in-law with every bit of financial information she had. She then agreed to listen to his advice and understand the consequences, both positive and negative. She wanted her financial plan to be a two-way relationship. "Probably having an education in that area, I was aware there were good and bad decisions you could make," she said of her accounting degree and MBA. "I saw people profligately destroy estates. I was willing to seek any counsel to not do that." Krieger seemed to care far less about the performance of her investments than her ability to maintain her lifestyle. She had little concern if her portfolio went up by 5, 10, 15 percent (or even if it fell), as long as she had enough money to live.

What Krieger didn't know at the time was that she was more than a mother-in-law in need of advice. She was client zero for a new company that would force clients to focus less on that most overused measure of investing success—returns—and more on all the other areas that determine if an investing strategy will actually succeed.

In investing, what separates the wealthy from the rich and everyone else? Brad Klontz, a financial psychologist who has an appointment to Kansas State University's personal financial-planning department, and I undertook a survey in the winter of 2013 to find out what was different about the One Percent. When it came to investing, almost all of them had a financial adviser, over 80 percent had an accountant, and two-thirds of them had a lawyer they consulted regularly. They would seem to be set. Yet those advisers could not protect them completely from the tendencies and biases that can derail anyone's investment strategy. One result in investing was that drawing the thin green line between the wealthy and the rich was not as simple as tallying up how much money someone had to invest. It isn't that easy. People with a lot of money to invest make the same dumb mistakes as everyone else. (They may, however, have more money to soften the blow of their bad judgments.) Just because they successfully managed businesses that sold cars or vinyl siding or computer software didn't mean they understood how to manage the money made from those decisions.

In our survey, with representative samples of people in the top 1, 5, and 20 percent for earnings, Klontz and I found that the One Percent were actually *more* likely than the top 5 percent to make common investing mistakes. They were overconfident in their investing ability. They made more trades. They took pride in selling winners, and they were more likely to hold on to investments that had lost value instead of selling them, taking the loss, and moving on to something else. They also invested in businesses run by friends—even though they said they knew that was a bad idea—and took friends' advice over that of a financial adviser on investments. (If this sounds acceptable, ask yourself how your friend whose day job is not investing money could possibly know more about what is happening with a particular company or the market in general than a professional money manager who focuses on this exclusively.) If the investments failed, they could, at least, admit they had made mistakes. While these findings make the One Percent similar to less rich people, it also shows how ingrained destructive investing behavior is. It almost seems hardwired.

Simple mathematics should cure anyone of these tendencies. People could run the numbers ahead of time and not take the risks that can be financially damaging. But most investors don't understand how percentages can go against you. A 50 percent drop in your portfolio—like ones many people experienced in 2008—requires a 100 percent increase to get back to even. That takes years. But even smaller drops require great returns to recover from. A 10 percent loss requires an 11.5 percent gain to get back to even; a 15 percent drop needs an 18 percent gain; and a 25 percent fall means the portfolio has to rise by a third. This is simple arithmetic that anyone can do, but it is far from obvious to most investors. It is the reason why people with a little try to invest aggressively to get a lot but can end up losing more than they can afford. They fail to realize that an investment that promised a 15 percent return can just as easily create a 15 percent loss or greater. The best anyone should hope for is a diversified portfolio with low fees and a positive return year after year.

But to be able to do this would be to act more like one of Thaler's economist friends than like a human. It would be hyperrational and discount any of the behavioral biases that have made Thaler's career. What people and their advisers need to do to get on the right side of the thin green line is to avoid the three things that can ruin any investment plan: optimism, trust, and self-confidence. When it comes to investing my own money, I shed these feelings, laudable in other areas of life, years ago. Being free of them has helped me get on the right side of the thin green line. I owe my skeptical view to three people: Gregg Fisher, Daylian Cain, and Terrance Odean.

Fisher, president of Gerstein Fisher, a wealth-management firm in New York, has found a way to get clients to be less optimistic without making them so pessimistic that they bury their money in the backyard. He is short and fit, with a shaved head and a large watch on his wrist. When I sat down in his office, amid the high-rises of midtown Manhattan, he extended to me a bowl filled with marbles.

"Without looking, pull one out," he told me.

I did. Black.

"Now put it back and take out another."

Black again.

"One more time."

White.

"You made money," he said with a smile.

In the bowl there were six white marbles and two black ones. The white marbles stood for a rising stock market; the black ones for a declining one. Historically, the stock market has gone up 75 percent of the time, but it doesn't go up three years in a row and down the next one. I had two declining years before I picked the white marble that meant my investments went up. What I didn't know was if they went up enough to recover from the two down years.

Fisher is smart, but more important he's curious. He manages $2 billion for about six hundred clients. His clients presumably think he knows more about investing than they do or they wouldn't have hired him. He plays down what he does.

"I'm the investment adviser and you're up nine percent for the year?" he said. "Big deal. There are larger issues." Such as how much you spend or how long you will live. But he said what his clients struggle with the most is being fixated on events that have already happened. That's the point of picking marbles out of the bowl: the color you just picked has no bearing on what color you're going to get next. "Most people cannot turn off yesterday," he said. "And if the past ten years are influencing your decisions around investing, it's going to hurt you." It works both ways. If you bought Apple stock at $100 and it went to $600, the rational thing to do would be to sell it: What is the likelihood that the stock is going to go up sixfold again? What he wanted to know, though, was if his rich clients were any better at resisting the urge to buy and sell at the wrong times.

In 2010, after seventeen years in business, Fisher thought he had seen a lot of bad investing behavior. To test his hypothesis, he decided to team up with Philip Z. Maymin, a former hedge-fund manager and professor of finance and risk engineering at NYU Polytechnic School of Engineering, to analyze his firm's clients. The two men focused on some 1.5 million client calls to Fisher's firm starting with its founding in 1993. After they weeded out the routine calls—happy holidays, here's my new address—they found that the number of calls to sell securities increased after down days in the stock market, while calls to buy securities increased after days when the stock market did well. If this behavior seems logical to you, then you're destined to lose money when you invest. A better strategy is to buy or sell a stock based on information about the future—a new product or a new market, a loss of competitiveness or an ineffective strategy—that could influence its price going forward. A savvier investor would take that information and decide what he thought the value of a stock should be and buy or sell it accordingly. While he would not panic because it went down one day—he might buy more because the lower price made it a deal—he would, just as importantly, sell the stock when it reached the value he thought it should have. Alas, the average investor acting on his own does not have this kind of patience.

The Maymin-Fisher study, which was published in the *Journal of Wealth Management* in 2011, found that the kind of knee-jerk reactions to what happened the day before cost an investor 4 percentage points of return each year. That's not only a drag on the portfolio but is difficult to recover from over time. What's more, there seemed to be no logical reason for people to call when they did. "It's more about the randomness of what they ate for lunch yesterday," Fisher said. "Or if they bought Google at the IPO, they're more likely to want to buy Facebook. That explains their risk behavior more." And people with more money called with the same frequency as people with less.

The study argued that the annual loss people suffered from their own folly was greater than the 1 percent an adviser charged to manage their money. That would sound like an argument for using an adviser, but the result presumed that advisers could hold themselves above the same urges that affected their clients. Don Phillips, president of investment research at Morningstar, which monitors mutual-fund performance, has questioned whether advisers can keep clients from making bad decisions. "If most investors use advisers and most investors continue to do the wrong thing, then there must be a tremendous amount of bad advice being given," Phillips wrote in a Morningstar report in October 2010. This was an argument for boring index funds that would be rebalanced without any input from the investors—a rational option that would help put you on the right side of the thin green line, but one that most investors struggle with because they think they can pick winners.

What I found equally interesting in the Maymin-Fisher study was the research that provided its hypothesis: a 1978 psychological study of a man who could not control his urges to binge-eat in the middle of the night. He went so far as to put a lock on his refrigerator and give the key to a friend. But he still woke up wanting to eat, unable to control the urge on his own. At some point the refrigerator would not be locked and he would binge again. Maymin made a similar observation about Fisher's clients—and investors in general: some cannot help themselves in buying high and selling low. "The urge never goes to zero," he said. "People who want to trade aggressively, it will never go away. If the market is volatile, it increases." An average investor might be better off thinking of that refrigerator, that urge to trade, as one of Thaler's fictional buckets called "retirement" or "college savings" or "winter vacation." He could mentally lock his money there and not touch it. It would be set aside for a goal and be as unretrievable as the money he spent on lunch. This strategy could keep him from caring about the price of the stocks day to day. Those movements would be irrelevant, and his chance of obtaining real wealth greater. It would make him less optimistic and in the long run wealthier.

Daylian Cain, an associate professor at the Yale School of Management, has focused on what advisers like Fisher tell clients when they call for all of their irrational reasons. Waving his hands in the air in a wood-paneled classroom as a photo was snapped, Cain looked as if he were doing the Monster Mash. But he might as well have been trying to frighten investors. His research has found that they are too trusting, particularly when their adviser tells them he has a conflict of interest. They generally don't understand the magnitude of the disclosure. Even if they did, they are still likely to invest in what the adviser tells them to invest in—even though he has just disclosed that the investment will benefit him. "Disclosure doesn't work because people don't understand that conflicts of interest are dangerous," Cain told me. "Even very clear disclosures don't actually have the intended warning effect. People stick to bad advice even when it's been disclosed. They adjust, but they don't adjust enough."

In the case of the adviser's disclosing a conflict, be it putting you into an investment run by his brother or one that pays him a higher commission, investors may buy less of what is being sold, but they will still buy some of it. They don't want their adviser to think they don't trust him or consider him dishonest. Simply put: investors do not understand the difference between what is being disclosed and what the risk is. "Warning that you're sitting on a plant is different from warning that you're sitting on poison ivy," Cain said. Or as Nicholas Stuller, the president and CEO of AdviceIQ, a company that evaluates advisers, said, what most investors say about their advisers has no correlation to a person's ability to advise them. "They'll always say, 'He's such a handsome man. He has a good golf handicap. And he's got a lovely family,'" Stuller said with a quick laugh. "These are utterly meaningless when it comes to picking an adviser. People don't know if he's a trust officer or a wealth adviser, an asset manager or fee-only planner."

A willingness to trust is good in other areas of life, such as marriage, but it may not be beneficial in investing. So what should you do when you don't understand what you are being told? Cain says it is impossible to get objective advice on anything to do with investing. For starters, if someone wants you to buy a stock because it is going up in value, that means someone else is selling it because they believe it has gone as high as it should—or maybe because the seller needs the money for something else and this is the best stock for him to sell. Investors need to ask themselves what incentives, financial or otherwise, their adviser has in telling them to buy or sell. It gets trickier. "We asked people how unethical it is to give potentially misleading advice to line your own pockets," Cain said. "Most people thought that was bad no matter what it was for." That's understandable. But then he added, "We asked another group that same question and said, 'But what if you disclosed your financial incentive in giving bad advice?' People thought it was okay."

This is what psychologists call moral licensing. Once you've disclosed your conflict of interest, the burden shifts, in this case, to the client who has been told and should be able to act prudently. But the research shows this will not be the case. The investor may make certain adjustments, but he will not adjust enough to account for the conflict. The solution would seem to be a second opinion from an adviser who has nothing to gain. But that fails, too. People demonstrate an anchoring bias, which means they use the first set of recommendations as the starting point. What they should do is collect many types of advice and weigh them against one another. "I think people need to consider how the advice they're getting is biased," Cain said. "It's not whether your adviser is corrupt. It's whether the advice you're getting is correct. Advisees need to work a bit harder to understand what they're getting."

This desire to trust, at the extreme, is why Ponzi schemes succeed. "We hear these ridiculous scams and wonder how people fell for them," Cain said. "But we're predisposed to listening to someone telling us something we want to believe, in this case about the investment being good. We're not good at taking an unbiased view of opportunity, particularly when they're coming to us with the investment." The best schemers know to target affinity groups—churches, neighborhoods, clubs—so that people see their friends getting something good and want in on it—or wonder why they haven't been asked. Bernie Madoff, after all, ran his scheme by targeting rich Jewish people he had come to know in New York and Palm Beach. They clamored to give him their money because their friends had done the same. These were people who at one point had enough money to be on the wealthy side of the thin green line, but they were trusting like the marks of petty schemers. Cain's advice? Procrastinate. "If the opportunity is gone tomorrow, it may mean that your money and your adviser could be gone tomorrow," he said. "There is no investment you need to make right now." Being a little less trusting could help your returns as much as getting that hot stock tip.

Making an investment after a conflict is disclosed is not a great idea, but other problems in buying are worse—like hearing about a company on TV while you're having lunch and buying the stock. Terrance Odean, a professor of finance at the Haas School of Business at the University of California, Berkeley, has done a series of experiments showing people are blithely and irrationally overconfident when it comes to investing and that our hot stock tips are rarely more than uninformed guesses. He had a hunch in the years between the tech-stock bust and the Great Recession that people overvalued their investment knowledge. His hypothesis was that stocks talked about on television would have a spike in trading on the day they were mentioned, regardless of the show or channel or person talking about the stock. He was right. In a 2008 paper, "All That Glitters: The Effect of Attention and News on the Buying Behavior of Individual and Institutional Investors," he labeled the television-driven stock-picking "attention-driven buying." With too many stocks for someone with a day job to choose from, investing in what flashed on the television screen narrowed the list of choices. "Buying is this daunting task," Odean told me. "Investors informally, if not consciously, limit their attention. The stock catches their attention and then they make the decision based on that. Instead of choosing from five thousand stocks, they consider fifteen." But the extent to which a television appearance of a stock sways investors' buying and selling habits is extreme. Odean wrote that the increase in desire to buy and sell stocks is measurable. On any given day at discount brokerages, the buy-sell imbalance for stocks out of the news is 2.70 percent and 9.35 percent for those in the news. At large retail brokerages it is more extreme: stocks outside of the news have a negative 1.85 percent buy-sell imbalance; those in the news have a positive 16.17 percent.

While it's comfortable for the investor and understandable, the gap shown by trading on television talk about stocks shows what a ludicrous way this is to spend your money. Without real research, how would you know the quality of those fifteen stocks? They could be fifteen great stocks, fifteen awful stocks, or a mix. Since you were probably eating lunch or otherwise taking a break from work when you caught the news, were you properly evaluating the tip, or just reacting like Fisher's clients? Is that person on television knowledgeable or is he trying to profit from what he is telling you without even the weak disclosures that Cain found do not work?

In his paper, Odean compared an individual's strategy with that of professional stock-pickers, who still pick losers but at least have a method. For one, they don't pick stocks based on seeing them on a business news show. "With more time and resources, professionals are able to continuously monitor a wider range of stocks," Odean wrote in the paper. They "are likely to employ explicit purchase criteria—perhaps implemented with computer algorithms—that circumvent attention-driven buying."

Of course, the alternative for an individual to choosing from a small set of stocks is to be totally overwhelmed by thousands of them and do nothing. But Odean's research has shown that it was unlikely people would take the time to pore through all the stocks; people prefer to divine patterns where none exist. "We're like pattern-finding machines," he said. "If lightning strikes and something falls off the table, we think the lightning caused it. Or worse, the book falls and lightning strikes and you think the book caused the lightning." Looking for patterns certainly has an evolutionary place: if you noticed family members being eaten by lions when they went out alone, you might not go out alone. But trying to divine patterns in stocks based on theories more akin to racetrack hunches is less likely to yield life-saving benefits. "The investor who is in the market and constantly seeing patterns better have a good day job," Odean said. Given that average investors lose money when they trade in and out of stocks, those investors who compound this behavior by buying stocks featured for whatever reason on television are doubly doomed.

So what about Odean? Was he immune to human frailty? "I buy index funds so when you ask me I can say that," he quipped. "People are overconfident about their ability to be an active manager."

But coming to that conclusion was hard-won. Before becoming an academic, Odean traded stocks between working at various day jobs. The result was not promising. "The thought that you can do part-time what professionals struggle to do full-time and with teams, that's hubris," he said. "Yes, I have a PhD in finance, but I don't think I can come home from work and spend an hour studying the market and do better than those guys at Goldman Sachs who do it all day long." He is also luckier than most people today: Berkeley has both a traditional pension plan and a defined-contribution plan that will make it easier for him to be on the wealthy side of the thin green line when he retires.

I met Jeannie Krieger's son-in-law Joe Duran at a fancy pastry shop in the Time Warner Center, which is essentially a high-end mall just off of Central Park in New York City. He had flown in from Newport Beach, California, where he lives and runs his financial advisory, United Capital. Duran had the good looks, easy smile, and black-rimmed eyeglasses that said, *Trust me.* I'm naturally skeptical of financial advisers, and his appearance did nothing to assuage that feeling. Add to it, his public relations guy, Jimmy Moock, had a name straight out of a David Mamet play and had been telling me that Duran was looking to be a different kind of adviser. Over the years, my feeling has been that people in finance who say they are doing something different, have done something different, or use the word *different* in any way related to how they invest money should be feared. The probability is high that they are wrong, lying, or simply not well versed in financial history. Most approaches to managing money, legal and illegal, have already been tried.

Sitting down with Duran, I was blasé without being rude. Yet within ten minutes, he had convinced me that he wasn't a huckster. His model leaned heavily on research like Thaler's that predicted human fallibility. In general, behavioral finance assumes that people, in their search for certainty, will look at the wrong things—to a stock going up or down, to a tip from a friend—and with that type of information, they can only make bad decisions. These decisions might not be bad that day, but since people keep making them, they add up. Over a lifetime, they compound into a big mess. Duran wanted to protect people from themselves. "We're not about performance," he said. "We're about good decisions." It is those decisions, many small, that add up and can put someone on the right side of the thin green line.

Duran's desire to help people make decisions is infused with the zeal of a convert. A native of Zimbabwe, at age thirty-five he sold his first company, a financial advisory firm. That money, from GE Financial, would have enabled him to do whatever he wanted or nothing at all. After a few years, he grew restless. As he helped his mother-in-law, he started thinking more about what his new firm, United Capital, could be. He knew that some people had some money but could not hire top-service firms with the best investment managers. Those advisers only worked with wealthy clients. People like his mother-in-law, with her "moderate, not mega, wealth," were the people he wanted to target. People with $200,000 needed to work and continue to save, he said, while those with tens of millions of dollars had access to the top advisers. He began United Capital to serve people who had $500,000 to $10 million, but to concentrate on clients with $1 million to $2 million. He planned to be discerning. He wouldn't take money from just any rich person. He would only manage money for people who pledged to take an active role in their financial future—who had a desire to be wealthy. He didn't want clients who pestered advisers about stock tips they heard from a friend or asked again and again where the stock market was headed; he wanted people who were thinking more about spending, saving, and, most of all, their ultimate goals.

Duran decided that spouses and partners had to come together to create and work through these goals. The passive person in the relationship had to express his or her financial opinion. This is easier said than done. So instead of trying to get people to talk, Duran invited them to play a card game. He called it Honest Conversations. Using three different decks of cards, it looked at people's financial fears, commitments, and the experiences that made them happy. At its most basic, it was meant to get people to stop thinking about stock market returns. On a higher level, it was meant to get people to contemplate bigger goals and fears—the way his mother-in-law thought about her portfolio as a source of funding her lifestyle, not as a scorecard. While returns—and the fees paid to generate them—were important in achieving the goal, the decisions people made based on emotions or assumptions were what could derail their investments and leave them on the wrong side of the thin green line.

"Honest Conversations will show you how your biases affect you," Duran said. "When you get to the whys of your biases, you get to a deeper place. You have to understand the consequences of your decisions and work on that. This is all about awareness."

This struck a nerve with me. I've committed many investing mistakes in my life. The first investments I ever made were in 1999 with a high school friend who worked at Merrill Lynch. We were both starting out. He had some thoughts about how I should invest the money. I had some different ideas. He didn't push back. A few years later, after I had told him to put all my money into technology stocks as the tech bubble was about to burst, I asked him to send me a check for what little was left. I'd bought high and sold with barely enough left to get a new pair of skis, boots, and poles. After that experience I tried to invest on my own, but I was overly conservative. My risk tolerance resembled my octogenarian grandparents'—a lot of low-yielding certificates of deposits that guaranteed my investment would still be there but not necessarily grow enough to keep up with inflation. After that I went with a big broker thinking he or his firm would provide a basic level of high-quality service. This idea came from my wife, who had someone managing her money—one of those guys recommended by a friend of a friend. He worked at Smith Barney, and we figured he must know something. And if he did not, the firm would have policies in place to make sure he didn't mess things up. The Eagle, as we called him, a play on his last name, talked a lot and had one idea he offered again and again: write covered calls, which makes a little bit of money but is to serious investing what pitch and putt is to tournament golf. I remember visiting him in his office on Park Avenue, which was in a corner with a good view of the skyline. He told us about having just visited the movie set of a director client, which I took to mean we should feel good to be in such company. When the market tanked in the summer of 2008, the Eagle was silent. Shortly after we lost 30 percent of our investment portfolio, we moved to a registered investment adviser we got to know while living in Boston. By then—or finally—we had wised up. As a true adviser—and not someone at a brokerage firm—he was bound by a fiduciary duty to act in our best interest. What sold us on him was his total lack of promises. Sure, he showed us possible returns, but he also told us how our spending and saving would affect those projections. He spent more time talking to us about considerations we had not properly addressed: insurance, tax planning, the costs of school and college, the vast and all-consuming money pit that a home could become. That was what we wanted—advice on all the things that we could control and confidence in his judgment on investments, which we couldn't. It was hard work for him and us.

Given my own history of investing, I wanted to play Duran's Honest Conversations. "Can you get one of your advisers to play the game with my wife and me?" I asked Duran.

A month or so later, Michael Duncan pulled into my driveway. Duncan was lean, short, and intense, with hair that was cut close to minimize its sparseness. His blue suit looked made to measure. As he walked to our door, he had a purpose in his step that was part doctor making an old-fashioned house call, part federal agent bearing a subpoena. Once inside, he wasted no time setting up his board game. My wife and I sat listening as he told us the rules and peeled off cards like a serious poker player—in lime green, slate blue, and what Duncan called papal purple.

"I invented this game," he told us. "I play it with all of my clients."

Despite his all-business demeanor and clipped speech, Duncan wanted to know what his clients wanted. Every adviser says this, but the game was a way for him to prove it. Duncan had had one particular client whom he had struggled to get through to—a cartoonist for the *New Yorker*, a magazine known for its oddball humor. The guy, he said, didn't want to look at charts and certainly did not want to read dry statements, so Duncan opted for something visual. "I thought the game would just be for curmudgeons in New York City who were difficult to talk to," Duncan said. "Then I did it with two of my best clients, and it changed how they looked at each other."

The cards address people's financial fears: "Protect my family if I am not around," "Have job and income security"; their various commitments: "Educating those I care about," "Minimizing taxes," "Supporting my charitable causes"; and the things that make them happy: "Personal growth," "Making work optional," "Doing what I've always wanted." My wife and I were each given our own deck of cards and told to pick out five cards and rank them in order of importance.

Before we started, Duncan gave us instructions as a judge would a jury: "These cards are not goals. These cards represent priorities." In case we didn't get it, he added, "Minimizing tax is not a goal. That's a priority."

He stared at us to make sure we understood. We got it. He gave us the okay to start. My wife and I were serious and guarded our hands like bridge champions. When we did the reveal, what we had shocked us all.

I consider my wife to be the risk-taker given her job in finance. She also has less fear when it comes to borrowing, spending, and investing money than I do. I would probably be called fiscally conservative, if not timid. I hate to buy anything on a credit card that I cannot pay off at the end of the month and would rather make investments where I can limit the losses even if that means giving up some of the gains. We were financial opposites. But the cards told a different story.

My wife's picks:

Spend time with the people I care about.
Protect my family if I'm not around.
Educate those I care about.
Prepare for the unexpected.
Improve/maintain health and wellness.

My picks:

Protect my family if I'm not around.
Spend time with the people I care about.

Educate those I care about.

Prepare for the unexpected.

Support other family members.

Only one card wasn't the same. My wife picked "Improve/maintain health and wellness," where I chose "Support other family members." That choice surprised her. It turned out that I had misunderstood it. Duncan said it was for my parents or cousins, not for my wife, children, or pets. I'm moderately close to my extended family—but I have no plans to support them later in life. Once I understood that, I dropped it. Why not wish I were healthier?

"I've only had one couple pick all the same cards," Duncan said. "They had been married for forty-two years." My wife and I had been together for eight.

But what did these cards mean for us? Like a good therapist, Duncan drew out our reasons. The first one, "Protect my family," meant having enough money to still live and educate our children if one or both of us died while they were young. This priority was the easiest, if most emotional, one to arrange: some term life insurance with reputable companies, a detailed will, and a guardian who shared our values for our children. The "Spend time with the people I care about" card should have been easy—just spend time with them—but it was harder to achieve. We told ourselves it was because our girls were young and we didn't have a lot of free time for our old friends. We figured we'd reconnect with them later. "Educate my children" was a combination of prudent management—saving as much as we could in 529 plans that allowed their college savings to grow tax-free—and hard thinking about the towns where we could live or the private schools we could pay to send them to. "Improving health and wellness" was the most aspirational. My wife signed up for classes in spurts. I liked to think of my level of fitness as middling—in a month's worth of exercise or neglect I could be fit or flabby. I worked out enough to maintain the status quo.

But those cards were relatively easy. The harder one, for me, was "Prepare for the unexpected." My wife saved because her parents had saved and it was the prudent thing to do. I saved because my parents had never saved yet wondered why they didn't have any money. I had lived through what it was like to be out of money at the end of the month and I didn't want that to ever happen again. I'm sure it's why I have so little patience for people who talk about money being evil: you can only think in those terms if you have enough of it or know nothing about its value. My problem, Duncan pointed out, was that I tended to go to an extreme. I wasn't cheap or even miserly; I just didn't like to spend money on unnecessary things. I was far happier having less stuff than more. But I drove a $55,000 Land Rover so it wasn't as if I were scrimping. (Land Rover rationalization: it was a safe car to drive our children in, and that is certainly true, though it was to safety what a fire hose is to a water pistol.)

"I've seen what can go wrong if you don't save," I told him.

Duncan, who drove up in a $60,000 BMW, said that people can go too far in the other direction. They could save too much and not enjoy themselves as they go through life. "There is a happy medium," he said. "The Dalai Lama says, 'We're not here to be unhappy.' That's what this process is all about, living your best financial life."

Had Duncan not been so buttoned-up, I would have burst out laughing at this Oprah-ish remark. But he had made an impression.

As Duncan walked out, he left us with another koan: "Your financial life is yours. Our job as financial advisers is to figure out how to make it work and, if it's not going to work, to say I don't think that's going to work."

A week later, unexpectedly, our results from a separate test we took with him arrived in the mail. The thin, manila envelope was the size of a college-acceptance folder with the weight of a rejection letter. Duncan wanted us to call him, like a doctor who has bad news but doesn't want to put it in a note.

On the phone, Duncan was less severe. His voice sounded deeper and more reassuring. We had passed, as it were.

"You're the weirdos," he said. "You'd be an easy client to work with because you're realistic. That's not normal. What's normal is people are a little bit unrealistic about what they expect in terms of returns."

We were going to be fine financially—something he said he did not often tell clients. But why us? What had changed so much in the time since my Tiger 21 meeting? We were savers and not spenders, he pointed out, but it was more than that: "You have a great long-term view. You have a partnership approach to everything and that's terrific."

Our goal is simple: to invest so we will be on the right side of the thin green line. We're trying to accomplish that by taking enough risk so our portfolio grows but not so much that investments lose all of their value and we have to make up a lot of ground. This approach is as much about the money we set aside to invest and don't touch as it is about the investments that money buys. This simple plan takes a lot of vigilance to achieve. It also requires that I tune out just about every offer to invest in the next great whatever, since most of those companies fail. And when I doubt it, I think back to the lessons of Fisher on optimism, Cain on trust, and Odean on self-confidence, and I invest a bit more in a broadly diversified portfolio and focus on what I can control.

3

DEBT AND THE
BORDEAUX DILEMMA

Darien, Connecticut, is a perfect coastal town. The homes are stately, the lawns and shrubs pristine. The area along the water, the neighborhoods of Holly Pond, Tokeneke, and Gorham's Pond, have extra cachet. But there isn't a bad place to live in a town where five-thousand-square-foot colonials costing several million dollars are the norm. The downtown is what downtowns are like in movies that take aim at the American dream: ice cream shops, pet and toy stores, restaurants from pub food to Thai, and a sprinkling of high-end national chains, such as Brooks Brothers and Ann Taylor. An old-fashioned playhouse offers a mix of blockbusters and children's movies. The people are not all perfect—I have seen short people around town and a few who could stand to lose three, maybe four pounds—but they might as well be: the men are athletically strong into their fifties, as if they were still college lacrosse players, and the women, whether pretty or plain, are all gym fit. If their children are not featured in catalogs for Tommy Hilfiger, Ralph Lauren, or Abercrombie & Fitch, they could be. The public education is great—not least of all because of the parents, with 95 percent being high school graduates and 70 percent having at least an undergraduate degree. College for their offspring is preordained; what is left is the pedigree of the degree, though anything less than a top-twenty-five school is a disappointment, even for parents who don't have an elite degree themselves. In the most recent census, from 2010, the town had 19,508 white people, 744 Asians, 743 Hispanics, and 104 black people. Ethnic diversity is not strong here. Nor is economic diversity: Darien is consistently ranked in the top-ten wealthiest towns in America, and the largest census group for earnings is people who make more than $200,000 per year. Even the area around the train station is nice. Probably nothing could make Darien any better for the people who live there, save being the first stop on the express train from New York. It is the third.

But, like all such towns, it has its dirty secrets, and I don't mean extramarital affairs or kids on drugs, which it has like any other wealthy town. Its secret is financial, which is fitting given that most of its wealth comes from people working at the upper end of financial services—bankers, lawyers, and a few hedge-fund managers. It's not an entrepreneurial town, unless you count losing your job in banking and starting a hedge fund as entrepreneurial. It's a meritocratic one, and finance is considered the pinnacle of achievement. Darien's dirty secret, though, is the same as what laid low all those striver towns in California, Nevada, and Florida: debt, loaded on and optimistically evaluated.

"To believe the majority of this community lives within their means is completely false," said Susan Bruno, a certified public accountant who grew up in Darien and returned after college. Bruno is fifty, blond, petite, and attractive in a way that makes her an archetype of a Darien woman. Today she is a financial planner, but she started out working as an accountant for Deloitte and PricewaterhouseCoopers. In Darien, she is an insider with an outsider's perspective when it comes to her neighbors' debts. In 2012 when we spoke, she was counseling many of her friends and neighbors on fixing their situations. Her advice is usually the same: sell the big house, buy a smaller one, stop wasting money. It is not, she said, what the people who ask her advice want to hear. Some, she claimed, end up fleeing town rather than be seen living within their means. "People move out of the community because they don't want to be in the same town where they downsized," she said, as if it were obvious why they'd rather leave than live in a measly twenty-eight-hundred-square-foot house.

I met Bruno at a restaurant called 1020, on the Boston Post Road, which runs through the center of Darien. She is pushy but charming. I wasn't surprised that she had married one of the town's star athletes, a man seven years her senior. She could be the town's mascot, allowing people who love or loathe Darien to project their feelings about the town onto her. On the plus side: She's smart and has the CPA to fend off any doubters. She runs her own business and raised two kids who by her account turned out okay: one graduated from a college in San Francisco and was working for a company Bruno had created in Austin, while the other was a student at Boston University. She had been married to the man she met at sixteen—he was twenty-three—for decades. On the minus side: She's gossipy in a shrewd way—prefacing salacious tales with "if you repeat this, my husband, who's Italian, will kill you." She's a name-dropper but a loyal one—a mere three weeks after Lance Armstrong was stripped of his Tour de France titles for using performance-enhancing drugs, she was telling me how she had done something for Lance and Sheryl (as in Crow, the singer and former Armstrong paramour), as if it were still good to be associated with him. She was also an expert in the dark art of slipping a connection to something prestigious into the conversation—from her relation to the founder of Fairfield University to her memberships at beach and golf clubs that I had never heard of but, she made clear, were coveted—and then immediately dismissing the value of such baubles of social standing.

She was, I was thrilled to say, the perfect mix of geek and gossip to guide me through Darien's overleveraged lanes. What she wanted to talk about was legitimately juicy: how so many of her friends and clients had gotten sideways with big, expensive homes with mortgages that were bigger and more expensive than what the homes were now worth. They were the rich, not the wealthy, of Darien.

When it comes to debt, drawing the thin green line is easy, but staying on the right side of it is not. Anyone who is wealthy is going to use debt sparingly or strategically to invest in a business or buy something that is going to appreciate in value, the way a home generally does over long periods. The rich and the poor are crowded together on the other side of the line, taking on too much debt for things they don't need, can't afford, and will only see lose value: clothes, expensive trips and dinners, fancy cars, excessive student debt for degrees that don't lead to jobs to pay back the loans, and houses that are too expensive for someone's income.

This happened in Darien the same way it happened in many less affluent towns. As house prices ran up in the 2000s, the big and beautiful homes of Darien went up in value, too. The rich of Darien did what everyone else in America did: they found mortgages that allowed them to buy the biggest house they could. In Darien—like many other wealthy towns where bonuses were four, five, ten times someone's six-figure base salary—people bought these glorious homes with an interest-only, adjustable-rate mortgage, or IO ARM for short. It came with the interest rate locked in for five, seven, or ten years, and that was the length of years people paid only interest. When that term expired, the rate reset and they paid principal and interest as with a regular mortgage. That moment was now looking like a bomb for some people as their payment would soon spike. This was not what they had thought would happen: home values were supposed to go up so people could refinance or more likely buy a bigger home in a more desirable sliver of this perfect town. If they had some home equity left over, they might spend it on a nice vacation to Turks and Caicos as if it were found money.

Bruno pointed out that when the rich of Darien were taking out IO ARMs, it seemed like a rational thing to do. People may have bought bigger homes that they could not otherwise have afforded with a traditional thirty-year loan, or they may have used the prospect of paying just interest to manage their cash flow, since bonuses came only once a year. But even doing that—with so many of those bonuses based on the discretion of a boss or, worse, a committee of bosses—put these people on the wrong side of the thin green line. They were using magical thinking to manage the debt on their home. Then the economy changed and expectations did not adapt. Most of the brokers pushing the IO ARMs did not foresee the real estate crash, and they certainly did not guess that it would be combined with a prolonged recession that would trim the ranks of highly paid financiers who live in places such as Darien just as surely as it did hourly wage workers in consumer-driven businesses. But when those two forces combined, the debt became burdensome. That $3 million house with a $2.4 million mortgage was suddenly worth $2.1 million, which meant it was underwater like so many other homes in America. Now when the interest-only period expires, the owner will either have to pay a much higher monthly mortgage bill or come up with $500,000 to have enough equity in the house to refinance it. If you made enough money to qualify for a mortgage on a $3 million house in the first place, it would seem that this shouldn't be a problem. That was not the reality.

People Bruno knows who made $2 million a year, for years, saved little if any of that money. Their house was not an investment; it was another lifestyle expense. To fund all of those expenses, people had borrowed against company stock or some other investment they didn't want to sell to get the down payment. Paying only the interest on the mortgage freed up cash to buy a new boat, a couple of fancy cars, a country-club or yacht-club membership, private-school tuition or at least tutors and then college fees for three, four, five children plus the annual donations to the schools' fund-raising efforts. The bonus could be used for a down payment on a second house at a far-off ski resort, plus a couple weeks of vacation. Since that $2 million becomes $1.2 million after taxes, those other lifestyle expenses pretty much used up what was a lot of money and may even have added to the person's debt. The interest alone on a $2.4 million loan at 5.5 percent was $132,000 a year. But the thinking—magical thinking—was that they would pay off debt with the next, even-bigger bonus. That day didn't come.

"Your status is more important to you," Bruno said. "You paid the country-club membership first because if you didn't have it, you weren't going to get hired when you lost your job. But now there isn't enough liquidity for people to refinance these mortgages."

I found her anthropological explanation of the inner workings of Darien reassuring and depressing. On the reassuring end, her stories of these people showed that the rich of Darien weren't that different from everyone else who was drowning in debt. On the depressing side, well, they weren't that much different from everyone else who dreamed of making the kind of money they did. Still, I asked Bruno, why would her friends balk at living in a smaller house that they could afford or own outright? It wasn't as if they were going to be moving in with their in-laws. Bruno did a double take. "You're expected to move up," she said as if I had asked Nigel Tufnel why his amplifier went to eleven when he could just have made ten louder. "If you don't move up, you're not successful. And you have to show that you're successful to get to the next level."

It would be easy to dismiss Darien as an anomaly. It is one in so many other ways, from the affluence of its residents to the achievements and aspirations of its children. So, too, was its view of debt management—treading not so much on the thin green line between wealth and richness but on a more precarious line between solvency and bankruptcy. But I take a different view: the rich of Darien—in their stately manors; clean, new luxury cars; and fine clothes named after rich people such as Peter Millar and Lilly Pulitzer—are no different from the low-income workers who bought too much house, lost it, and were excoriated for bad decision-making. While some of the people of Darien may have had a reasonable expectation that their bonus would stay high or even grow, for most it was irrational. They could have used some time with Steve L., the Tiger 21 member who told me that our view of the future did not match up with how we were living our life today. We were spending too much to be able to pay for the life we expected to live, even though we weren't in any financial jeopardy at the time. This statement was more universal than he imagined.

Mark R. Rank, a professor of social welfare at Washington University, and Thomas A. Hirschl, a professor of development sociology at Cornell University, examined forty-four years of data on a group of people aged twenty-five to sixty to prove it. They were trying to determine how people's income fluctuated. They found that 12 percent of Americans would be in the top 1 percent and 39 percent would be in the top 5 percent for at least one year in their life. Over half would crack the top 10 percent—with an income greater than $115,000 a year—during their lives. But those years wouldn't last. Their riches—in this case their income—would fade. The only ones who could be secure were those who had wealth—in the form of savings, investments, and more equity than debt in their homes. "While many Americans will experience some level of affluence during their lives, a much smaller percentage of them will do so for an extended period of time," Rank wrote in an opinion piece in the *New York Times*. To wit, only 0.6 percent of Americans will be in the top 1 percent for ten consecutive years. People will have good years and bad years, which is obvious even though it could at times during the Great Recession seem that only farmers, at the whim of the weather and crop prices, understood this point. Rank also cited the work of Robert Carroll of the Tax Foundation, who found in Internal Revenue Service data that half of the people who earned more than $1 million between 1999 and 2007 did so for just one year; only 6 percent did it for the entire period. They were surely rich for a year or two, but few had the chance to parlay those high salaries into wealth. Income, the data showed, was unstable at the top as well as the bottom.

But even if you did not know about Rank's work, the Great Recession showed that the rich of Darien were not alone in being seduced by debt. Across the country, in the hot Arizona desert, the affluent people of Phoenix were equally enamored of the IO ARM. "When the recession hit in 2008, we got hit superhard," said Armando Roman, a certified public accountant and financial adviser in Phoenix. "People who took out five-, seven-, ten-year ARMs got stuck. The value of their property dropped tremendously and they were upside down." Now, to be rich in Phoenix does not require as much money as it does in Darien: the average price of a four-bedroom house in Phoenix, according to Trulia, was under $388,642 in 2014; it was $1.8 million in Darien. But the same dynamics were at play back then: people embracing debt as if it were a dream. In Phoenix, dreaming was not such an irrational idea. Arizona laws allowed people to walk away from their mortgage. "The whole idea of being a little more conservative and not stretching your neck out so far, I don't know that that has left the mark on people that it should have," Roman told me. "They could get the identical house on their street for half the price of what they owed on the last house. They simply walked away from the home." He emphasized that the people who made these choices were "educated, high-income people" who could take the emotion out of their decision and calculate that it made no sense to live in a house where the mortgage was more than what the house was worth. Plus, their life didn't change if they moved across the street. It worked for them, as the saying goes. And like a mirage in the desert, their bad choices disappeared.

Most people cannot walk away from their mortgage worry-free. Therefore, how people manage their debt is far more important than how they invest their money. The burden of debt can turn quickly against someone; it is an equal-opportunity destroyer of wealth, if not lives. Of the estimated $11.4 trillion in total consumer debt in America, $8 trillion of that debt is in mortgages. The average American with a median income of $52,762, according to the US Census Bureau, owes $47,000. (A third of that debt is on credit cards.) The Consumer Federation of America issued a report in the winter of 2014 warning that only a third of Americans were living within their means and not encumbered with debt that would impede their future. It said another third were not spending beyond their means but they weren't prepared for a future in which expenses—expected or otherwise—could arise. The last third were struggling. For people who owned homes, the situation was worse. In 2010, the Consumer Federation asked people about the debt on their homes, and 68 percent said they were building equity; in 2014 that percentage had fallen to 54 percent. The number of people who expected to pay off their mortgage before they retired had also fallen: 78 percent in 2010 said they would have it paid off, but only 68 percent said they planned to do it when asked in 2014. Owning a home in the second half of the twentieth century was a way for the middle and upper-middle class to build wealth. After paying a mortgage for thirty years, people would either have something that would serve as their backstop if they ran out of money—such as my grandparents who, when they grew infirm, sold their house so they could move into an assisted-care facility—or something they could sell so as to move somewhere where lower home prices could support their retirement. But it was not something people gambled with: they paid their mortgage first. Then came the housing boom in the 2000s and so many people crossed the thin green line into bad choices on debt.

Why did this shift occur? The Consumer Federation suggested people had abandoned their spending and savings plans. That could be true, but if people were not building equity in their homes or were unable to pay off their mortgages before they retired, then they were living in homes they could not afford. In the research Klontz and I did on the spending habits of the One Percent and the Five Percent, we found that the wealthy and the rich spent about the same portion of their income on housing—22 to 24 percent—and that their spending was roughly the same as a percentage of their income in almost every category, including credit-card debt, vacations, philanthropy, and their children. The two exceptions were eating out and saving for retirement. Of their income, the One Percent spent 30 percent less eating out and saved 30 percent more for retirement. Over years those differences become enormous.

The one person I know who has bought his house—homes—the right way is an unlikely role model for anything. I'll call him Carl given his well-founded aversion to publicity. Life has been good to Carl. He was born affluent—his father invented a type of car trim that every automobile manufacturer wanted for a time and took home millions of dollars a year from the 1950s through the 1970s. A sustained windfall like that gives a man's children options. Carl's sisters have done nothing but sue each other and him. Carl's become wealthier running an unsavory media company: he collects broadcasting fees from people who make money off poor people. He's a toll collector, providing a platform—satellite, Internet, radio—to people who want to get their message out. He is happy to let anyone onto his highway without peering into the car window to see what is going on. Even if he did peek, I don't think what he saw, however egregious, would matter to him. He just collects his toll.

A mutual friend introduced Carl and me. Carl wanted someone to hang out with while his wife was shopping; I wanted to hear his stories. On a winter day in Naples, Florida, he took my wife and me out on his eighty-five-foot yacht. We cruised a couple of miles offshore in the Gulf of Mexico. A rare Italian design, the boat cut smoothly through the slight chop. The sun was warm without being hot. I was eating stone-crab claws and drinking a cool pinot grigio regularly refilled by the captain's wife. The afternoon was as relaxing as life could get. Carl started telling me how financially conservative he was. At first I thought he was delusional. We were burning thousands of dollars of fuel going nowhere fast. I also knew that Carl has four homes—in Naples, Park City, Los Angeles, and the town where he grew up. He also has forty-seven cars, including a Rolls-Royce Phantom, Bentley Continental GT, Jaguar convertible, and beach-ready Jeep in his Naples driveway. The only concession to frugality I ever detected was his use of a NetJets membership instead of having his own private jet. Carl lived large. But as he spoke, I realized it wasn't quite as large as it could have been: he lived below his enormous means.

"I have so little debt," he told me. "I hate debt. I've got so much risk in my business that I'm invested in Treasuries."

What about the houses? He said two of the four were free and clear—including the one in Florida, which is protected under the homestead law if he ever lost a big lawsuit. Together those two houses were worth $12 million. The other two each had a $500,000 mortgage on them, since $1 million was the limit for interest on mortgages to be tax deductible. Those houses were worth another $9 to $10 million. "If I ever lose it all, my wife and daughter can sell one of the houses and the cars and live fine," he said. As for the cars, they were bought with cash through a buyer who worked for him. This might seem odd, but the buyer protected Carl from getting caught up in the emotion of the moment and spending more on a car than he should. If the car got bid up at auction, the buyer didn't have the authority to chase the price; he had to let it go. Only the yacht, Carl said, had any debt on it. He claimed it was better to own it that way. I didn't know enough about mega-yacht ownership to argue about it.

Unlike many of the folks in Darien, Carl is his own boss. He is not working for a bank or a brokerage, nor is he a hedge-fund manager, who is wholly dependent on other people's money to execute his wild strategies and collect the high fees that go with them. Carl has a company that provides a service, and he runs it as leanly as possible. He was proud of how few employees he had, about thirty, and prouder still that his business, with a footprint on every continent, was debt-free. That mattered to him. What mattered less was making a difference in the world, which he would never say he was doing. What he loved was the efficiency of his company. It was also wildly profitable.

Most people don't think about their personal profit margin the way Carl did. But anyone who has used the term *nut* to refer to the monthly or yearly minimum one needs to cover before one can start saving or have some fun is thinking about it. Carl took it a step further. Even though he did a fine job of spending millions of dollars a year, he also made sure that he socked away money in case his business failed. He planned to sell the company one day and retire early. He liked the idea of becoming a professor and holding forth on what he knew, even though he had been an awful student. But he knew being asked to lecture somewhere was not in his control, and even if he could do it, the pay would be insignificant compared to what he was making. He needed safe money. That was the Treasuries, paid-for homes, and exotic cars.

What is striking about Carl is how ordinary his personal and professional life were despite his enormous fortune. If you saw him on the street, with his Gucci loafers, large-face watch, and T-shirt with his yacht's name on it, he could be any overleveraged financier in Darien. But he isn't: Carl is wealthy.

Now, it's easy to dismiss someone like Carl because of the size of his wealth. How could he ever run out of money? It would seem that he couldn't, but many like him have. Patricia Kluge's high-profile divorce in 1990 from John Kluge, who made billions in television, radio, and outdoor advertising, gave her the title of "richest divorcée in America." Her divorce settlement was supposedly worth $100 million. (At the time, he was worth over $5 billion, which made him the richest man in America.) She should have never had a financial care in the world. But in June 2011, she filed for Chapter 7 bankruptcy—that's the kind where you admit total defeat as opposed to Chapter 11, where you try to rebound. She claimed debts up to $50 million and assets of no more than $10 million. News reports said much of that debt was incurred from some $66 million in loans to expand a vineyard she built in Charlottesville, Virginia, with her current husband. In the recession, Kluge could not sell enough wine to make the loan payments, fell behind, and essentially faced foreclosure like any number of other Americans. Donald Trump, a friend, bought the vineyard and gave her a job running it. After a year, he fired her.

When we were looking to buy our house in the spring of 2008, the mortgage broker said we were approved for a loan so large that we were standing in the eight-thousand-square-foot house of a senior executive at ABC Sports. (The Realtor let us know what the owner did, perhaps to keep us from wondering who the overweight, bald guy was in all the pictures of famous athletes.) The house was in New Canaan, not too far from David Letterman's old house—the one that the stalker kept appearing at. The sportsman's house was new, clean, and beautiful and had all the things that are costly to change: perfect kitchens and bathrooms, no weird rooms or oddly angled walls. It was also hidden on many acres in the woods. We couldn't believe we could afford it, but the broker said we had the income to pay the mortgage—an interest-only loan with the rate set for ten years. When we calculated the monthly payments, we weren't as confident as she was: it would have taken more than half of our after-tax income for just the mortgage, leaving us hoping for big windfalls to pay for everything else. When we brought this up to the Realtor, she told us it was better to buy a big house that we could grow into. We were two people with two dogs. How many kids would we need to fill eight thousand square feet?

We passed, and I'm glad we did. Our quick math took taxes into account but not all the other expenses that go along with owning a house, such as lawn care, sprinkler service, pool maintenance, snow removal, and the highly paid tradesmen—electricians, plumbers, arborists, and painters—that show up throughout the year. Yet a bank would have given us a giant mortgage if we had wanted it. Part of what held us back was what we knew from growing up. My wife lived in a typical 1980s house in suburban Atlanta—maybe thirty-five-hundred square feet, on an acre or so, with similar houses all part of a neighborhood association. Her father, a dentist, knew how to maintain the home and the yard. They made friends and led a comfortable life. I grew up in rental apartments and a condo. I knew nothing about the work that went into owning a home. My only experience with a house had been with my grandfather's home. I cut his front and back lawn, which together were probably a tenth of an acre. But a bigger part of what held us back was what my wife and I had learned through Manhattan's often maligned and always stressful co-op boards. Both of us had gotten the approval to buy the co-op apartments we owned before we met. (She was turned down for one apartment when a board member pulled out a scale to weigh her dog, which ended up being over the building's weight limit.) It's an easy process to ridicule: you, the buyer, have to submit intimate financial details to a board that will determine if you can buy an apartment in the building, even though a bank has already approved you for the mortgage to do so. I hated it when I went through it, afraid that they would deny me because of how I looked or answered their questions. But I think about it differently now. Judging from the characters in every New York apartment building, the boards could not care less how you look. They care that you have the means to pay your mortgage and just as important your monthly maintenance bill, because if you fall behind on that, the rest of the co-op has to pay your share. The board looks at how much you are putting down as a deposit and also at how much you have left over as a cushion. Under these rules, my wife and I were allowed to spend only so much on our first apartments without the boards' rejecting us. While this seemed constricting at the time, in retrospect it taught us moderation.

Out in Connecticut in 2008, as the boom started to fizzle, we could have bought that big house and moved right in—with our two-bedroom apartment's worth of furniture. For a while my wife talked about the house and wondered if we had made a mistake. Then the financial world collapsed. Like many who survived, we had to make quick and serious adjustments to our spending and saving. Having manageable debt was key to being able to move nimbly. That house would have been a burden for years. The mortgage broker and real estate agent, who would have received bigger commissions had we acted otherwise, were baffled by our uncharacteristic frugality. But we carried with us the lessons from the co-op boards: they had instilled in us a sense of limits. We ended up with something far from a shack, a smaller house in Stamford on a slightly smaller plot of land for considerably less. But it still had a pool, nice backyard, and a good deal of extra space. The upkeep is not cheap, but we've never felt strapped owning it. We didn't deprive ourselves. Having learned restraint facing a co-op board, we made decisions that preserved our freedom. The co-op board covenant, at its most basic, requires people not to take on so much debt that they let their neighbors down. In the housing boom, any sense of restraint was lacking. It was catch-as-catch-can. Buyers tried to get the most house they could, convinced that they would be missing out otherwise. Banks were happy to lend on those dreams because they could sell the mortgages to investors who still believed that people took the responsibility of owning a house seriously and would always pay their mortgage. These assumptions were untrue. No person better summed up the mood than Chuck Prince, the chief executive of Citigroup, who said he wasn't worried about the subprime-loan crisis and wouldn't be until he had to. "When the music stops, in terms of liquidity, things will be complicated," he said, in a now-famous piece that appeared in the *Financial Times* while I worked there. "But as long as the music is playing, you've got to get up and dance. We're still dancing." Five months later, as the music started to sound warbled, he was replaced.

Overindulgence with debt is certainly not confined to home buying. Most people are susceptible to what I call the Bordeaux Dilemma. Bordeaux is one of my favorite wine regions in the world, and I have wonderful memories of drinking some of the great wines from that part of France, particularly Château Margaux, which can entice me to spend $300 or more on a bottle. Bordeaux is as seductive to me as debt is to other people: I certainly can't have just a little bit. But at times I've wished I had never drunk Château Margaux or any of the region's other great wines. Once you have, your taste buds are changed forever. That $20 bottle of wine will never taste the same, and that $80 bottle in the restaurant will prompt you to remember that time, so long ago, when you sat at a different table and ordered the Margaux. That's the Bordeaux Dilemma, a desire to drink that wine all the time, but the knowledge that it would limit your ability to pay for more essential things in life. Any premium item can induce the same feeling, from fine food to luxury cars to the feel of a bespoke suit. These things *are* better than their mass-produced, less expensive versions, and once you've had one, it's hard to return to what once seemed just fine. I know only three cures for this: poverty, incredible wealth, or self-restraint mixed with occasional indulgence. This last is a great balancing act, and the key to being on the right side of the thin green line.

My old friend K. Dun Gifford, a great food enthusiast and the founder of a food think tank called Oldways, advocated "management not banishment" when it came to food and drink. Dun, a Boston Brahmin, understood human nature, inherited some money and made some money, and hung out with Kennedys, Rockefellers, and Harvard professors. He knew that telling people not to have a can of Coke or McDonald's french fries was a losing battle—not least of all because he used to bring McDonald's fries to his friend the fabled chef Julia Child, who would whip up a martini to drink with them. He got the idea for Oldways—from the notion that we should eat and drink as our ancestors did—after a thirty-course meal in Shanghai, where every course was paired with a thimble of alcohol. In the haze of what he called his "mai-tai hangover," Oldways was born. He advocated big nights like that, but he knew they had to be balanced with a couple days of more moderate eating and drinking. A favorite antidote was a crisp green salad with fine olive oil, because the fat in the olive oil would trigger satiation. And there would still be occasion for that Bordeaux.

When it comes to debt, I think like Dun. The only viable solution is to create a plan with moderation, not abstention. People can't live in voluntary deprivation. Any debt solution is about arithmetic and the battle against compounding interest. Others have suggested paying off credit-card debt card by card. If that helps, great. It's bucketing, and it might work. A more rational plan might be to figure out what you earn each month after taxes and then write down all of your essential expenses: rent or mortgage, transportation, food, any medicines you might need. If you took what was left and put it all toward the credit-card debt, you would be on a diet doomed to failure. You need a more balanced approach where your monthly payment is reducing the debt—not just paying interest—yet you still have money for fun. Rather than swearing off debt one morning and announcing your epiphany to everyone you know, taking a more moderate approach will get you to a healthier place. The latter is management, not banishment.

Of course, some people are debt-free. For them, the question is not just how to stay that way but how to benefit from that rare position, as Carl has, and save so that the future will be what you want it to be. To do so requires a wholesale reimagining of how you think about the value of debt. Even those people should still keep all the essential costs on paper and figure out what they think they will need to save for the big expenses in life—college for kids, retirement. You can then divide the contributions toward those goals equally or create a sliding scale and contribute less in the beginning and more as your income grows. Then spend no more than what you have left, even if you have to wait until the next month to buy something. No excuses. You'll avoid debt and the stress of debt. You might also enjoy what you buy more because you had to think about it.

I had initially thought that Bruno was an unlikely evangelist to help the have-mores rein in their debt-fueled ways. She should have been out there on the tennis courts with them. But over drinks, I realized that as a product of this town, she had her own struggles. She repeatedly found a way to tell me that her house, along the water, was small (thirty-five hundred square feet) but worth $3 million. (A Zillow search later told me it was worth half that amount.) She said that she and her husband were secure but admitted that their standing in town had been helped by his athletic glory, even though it had been thirty years since his greatness had bloomed. But her plan to help those in debt was targeted. She was most concerned with helping women understand their finances after their husbands had landed the family in a real jam. This would have been the result of one of the five D's: death, divorce, disaster, disability, and debt. Of these, she made clear that the only one that doesn't trouble people as it should is debt. For death, disaster, and disability, there was insurance, and divorce in this world was a business transaction, although costly. Debt was the elephant in the room, present but never spoken about. "The younger wives don't want to know," she said, "and the older ones are petrified to know." She shared one success story: the couple sold their big house, moved to a different town to save face, and stayed married. Not exactly *Love Story*. Yet when she brings out her CPA side, Bruno is more helpful. She likes to convince clients to let her run a stress test on their debt. It's a great idea, because if investing is dreaming about the future, managing debt is coming to terms with the past and its impact on the present and everything else.

As our conversation was wrapping up, Bruno slid a couple of sheets of paper across the table, like an informer in a spy movie. The restaurant was dark by now so I couldn't read them, but she explained that the numbers were real, though a few details had been changed so the client wouldn't know it was his financials she was passing along. When I looked at the papers later, I saw that he had a nice home in Greenwich, worth $8.4 million, and a ski home in Vail worth $3.75 million. On the Greenwich home, he had a $1.7 million mortgage as well as a $1.25 million home-equity line of credit. This meant only 35 percent of the home was mortgaged, which seemed good. His annual payments on the two loans were $55,625. On the Vail home, the mortgage was $2 million, which was a loan-to-value ratio of 53 percent, still respectable. The annual payment on that loan was $113,000—for a grand total of $168,625 in annual debt payments on homes. That's a lot, but presumably he made a lot, too. He also had two margin loans on securities in brokerage accounts, one at the maximum of 51 percent and the other at 28 percent of the account value. Then he had a $1.1 million loan for half the value of a business mortgage. All three taken together totaled another $80,000 in annual payments.

For him, the stressful part would come when interest rates rose on his debt. A half percentage point increase on the home debt would increase the annual payments by 14 percent, Bruno said. A

1 percentage point increase would raise them by 30 percent. If you got to a 3.5 percentage point increase in interest, the annual payments would double—and remember those payments only covered interest, not principal. Such an increase was easy to imagine: in the aftermath of the Great Recession interest rates were down under 3 percent from the pre-2008 levels of close to 7 percent. There was no reason they would not go back up. The same would happen with the business loans, though the other risk was that the value of the margined securities would go down. That could require him to pay back money he had borrowed. In this fragile situation a couple of events beyond his control could crush him financially.

"The bonus was always supposed to pay down the principal, but it went to lifestyle expenses," Bruno said. "This is a house of cards for many people."

Even if he is okay, if this scenario doesn't come to pass, the mentality that allowed her client and so many other people to take on so much debt remains. They're dangling on the thin green line—if not in free fall from it—when they should be some of the most comfortable and wealthy people in America. This lapse in judgment is where the rich are often living lives with debt that are just as shaky as middle- and working-class people who get maligned for making ludicrous purchases. They are all suffering from the Bordeaux Dilemma. With just a little bit of restraint with their debt, particularly among the rich of Darien, who could still live fantastically well with less, they would be on the right side of the thin green line. If that restraint proved unnecessary, the only downside would be that they would end up with a bit more money left over for savings.

4

THE FUTILITY OF FRETTING ABOUT TAXES

In a real estate listing, Brad Birkenfeld's summer accommodations would have sounded great: "waterfront condo with uninterrupted ocean views on the exclusive South Shore, marina, quick ocean access, just 30 minutes from downtown Boston." In 2008, he could have used a peppy Realtor to spruce up his situation. When I drove to Weymouth, Massachusetts, to talk to him, he was a federal witness under house arrest. His life was bleak. Earlier that summer, he had been arrested at Logan Airport as he entered the country to attend his high school reunion. He had been able to strike a deal with the government to tell everything he knew. In return he got to stay in his brother's condo with the water view, not in a cell where he would stare at a wall. I had been with Birkenfeld in Fort Lauderdale a month earlier when he was being arraigned. Dressed in a dark suit and white shirt with closely cropped hair and a goatee, he looked bloated and a bit lost. Yet he wasn't in court for killing someone, smuggling drugs, or even stealing state secrets. He was there for helping a fantastically rich guy—who should have seen himself as well on the wealthy side of the thin green line—avoid paying taxes. Birkenfeld had been a jet-setting international banker but had risked his freedom and his liveli-hood to help someone with hundreds of times his wealth cheat the Internal Revenue Service. What did he get in return? A bonus from the bank that employed him and a few nice trips? It seemed like an awful deal to me.

Birkenfeld had grown up on the affluent South Shore of Boston, the son of a neurosurgeon, which I thought was ironic in the months I trailed him. He just didn't seem that smart. He had left the United States over a decade before to seek his fortune in Switzerland, where he acquired the trappings that a lot of money can buy. He had an apartment on the Cours de Rive, in central Geneva, where he lived during the week, and a weekend home in Zermatt, at the base of the famed Matterhorn. In contrast, his brother's condo looked as if it had been designed by a brutal Soviet architect; the concrete apartment buildings were set parallel to each other in a way that made them seem as if they were attacking the water. The only road into the com-plex led through a grimy boat-repair shop with old fishing boats up on concrete blocks. The gatehouse of the complex looked as if it were meant to keep residents in, not visitors like me out.

How Birkenfeld had ended up here was a lesson in why it is unadvisable to try to outsmart the Internal Revenue Service. Those on the right side of the thin green line find ways to pay exactly what they owe; those on the other side think they have concocted ways to pay less than that. And while the wealthy may get audited, far worse downsides exist for playing cute with the IRS. Birkenfeld had had an undistinguished career in finance that was consistent with a life of minimal work and maximum reliance on his father, who had the money to help him along. (His father had sent him to a small military college in Vermont to shape up, but Birkenfeld skated through by bragging about his family's money and never took a military commission, which some of his classmates told me was looked at dishonorably.) In the 1990s, he left Boston for Switzerland and his career changed, like that of the kid who switches schools and reinvents himself. Birkenfeld attended a business school that had just opened and worked his way up to a job at UBS, the biggest private bank in Switzerland and among the biggest financial institutions in the world. He worked in the part of UBS's private bank that catered not just to wealthy people, as all private banks do, but to wealthy people who wanted their money shielded by Switzerland's strict banking laws. There are noble reasons for having a secret Swiss bank account—say if you were an African human-rights campaigner fearing your country's government might seize your assets to silence you—but Birkenfeld worked on the ignoble side, for incredibly rich American citizens who didn't want to pay US taxes.

Birkenfeld's biggest client was a Russian immigrant named Igor Olenicoff, a whale who had made a fortune in real estate and kept $200 million with Birkenfeld and away from the worldwide taxing power of the United States. (Olenicoff would later plead ignorant to the charges and complain that he was just following UBS's advice in not paying tax.) That one account ensured that Birkenfeld kept his job. But after four years, his superiors grew frustrated with his mediocre performance. He hadn't landed any other whales. They gave him poor reviews and cut his bonus as a hint for him to leave, and he eventually did. On his way out he called Olenicoff and convinced him to move his tax-avoiding account to a small bank in Lichtenstein. Still, Birkenfeld was bitter. He decided to tell the Internal Revenue Service about what had been going on at UBS. That he had been complicit in what had happened seemed not to dawn on him. He had not merely overheard plans to hide money; he had done the hiding. In addition to everyday management of a tax-evading account, Birkenfeld had smuggled diamonds in a toothpaste tube from Switzerland to California, where Olenicoff lived. Unbeknownst to Birkenfeld, Olenicoff was under investigation when he moved his account to Lichtenstein, so federal authorities caught both men evading taxes.

Birkenfeld had landed in his brother's depressing condo not from one bad choice, but a series of them. But what I couldn't stop thinking about was, why would anyone risk his career and his freedom for a salary of a couple hundred thousand dollars a year to help someone worth billions save a few million in taxes? A $200 million account should have generated a return of $15 million a year, more than enough to pay the $7.2 million Olenicoff owed in taxes. Yet Olenicoff had taken the risk and Birkenfeld had aided him. Now both were living by the water, though Olenicoff did not have an ankle bracelet in his mansion in Newport Beach, California.

When I was eighteen or nineteen, I received a letter from the Internal Revenue Service informing me that I was being audited. I was furious. The last thing I was doing was cheating on taxes. Everything I earned came from my summer job at a golf course—which deducted all of my taxes. I had no investments and no family money. I was on financial aid to college, with loans to boot. I had a negative net worth. My response befit a college freshman in full: an over-the-top mix of contempt and arrogance flowed into my letter back to the IRS. If I remember right, I handwrote the response. It let the IRS know what a complete waste of time and taxpayer dollars their investigation of me was. I pointed out that as a financial-aid student, I was pretty much broke. If I had cheated the IRS, it would have been inadvertent and small since I wasn't making enough to pay a lot in taxes anyway.

I didn't know it at the time, but all of my summer paychecks were reported directly to the IRS, so they didn't have to take my word for what I earned. A few months after I sent my letter off, I received a response from the IRS saying my case had been closed. I would never claim victory against that agency, for fear of waking its ire. But I was relieved.

That letter was an early and scary lesson: the IRS is one of the few government agencies that can make your life miserable on a whim. I can imagine the Federal Bureau of Investigation hassling people for nothing, and the National Security Agency could be listening to my phone calls and reading my e-mails for all I know. But most agencies need a reason to come after you: if agents from the Bureau of Alcohol, Tobacco and Firearms kick in your front door, chances are the CNN trucks have been parked across from your house for days. But the IRS can, with a simple letter, make you prove that you didn't cheat on your taxes, even though they are sending that letter on a hunch generated by a computer program.

So I pay my taxes on time. I consider them the price of living in a stable, civilized country. I believe that people who try not to pay their taxes are misguided: you have so many ways to pay exactly the tax you owe—which is lower than you would think—but few legal ways to avoid taxes entirely, short of dying with a bunch of appreciated stock and property. Whether poor, rich, or wealthy, people love to complain about taxes, and the complaint is almost always the same: they pay too much and get too little, at least of what they want. (I have yet to hear someone say, "I pay so little in taxes for all these services that make my life easier.") But complaining is all most people can do because no one has any control over how the tax rate is set and the taxes spent. Some people boast about their refund, but that shows a misunderstanding of how taxes work: that refund check was their money, lent to the Treasury Department interest-free.

A wealthy few, though, are the professional baseball players of minimizing taxes, with accountants and attorneys who ensure they pay exactly what they owe and not a penny more. If they pay a little less and get audited, they pay the tax, a small penalty, and keep playing, like getting thrown out while trying to steal second base. Then there are people like Olenicoff and their enablers like Birkenfeld. They are akin to baseball's steroid-fueled home-run kings. They go to the edge of legality and juice right over the line. They know what they are doing is illegal, but they are confident that they can outsmart the authorities. This last group is the image that many people have of wealthy taxpayers: cheats, crooks, and scoundrels. In reality most of them are like Carl, intent on paying as little tax as they legally can, but aware that they will be audited regularly and always have their documents in order. That Carl, with his hundreds of millions of dollars in wealth, may pay a lower percentage of his income—though a higher dollar amount—than middle-class people may not be fair, but it's not illegal. In this, he is not all that different from those Darien people who are allowed a tax deduction on their mortgages up to the first $1 million. It's the way the tax code is written, which is a bigger issue than any one taxpayer could ever address.

But when it comes to establishing the thin green line for taxes, it takes either rugged determination and great wealth to pay attorneys and accountants to figure out how to reduce your tax bill to its minimum or resignation that taxes cover the costs of the services we need, such as safe neighborhoods, paved roads, and public schools, even if they also pay for things that we individually wish they didn't. Those on the other side of the line are trying to game the system or neglecting what they owe as if the tax collector will not come after them. With taxes, the wealthy stand out in three areas, involving long-term thinking about what we can control, not griping about the rates that are set at the state and federal levels.

First, wealthy people know better than to listen to people like Warren Buffett about taxes. When he talks taxes, the great investor speaks nonsense. In the summer of 2011, he wrote an opinion piece in the *New York Times* boasting about his low tax rate—a mere 17.4 percent. (This still amounted to $6.9 million in taxes.) The highest income-tax rate was then 35 percent, but Buffett paid so little because most of his earnings were from capital gains on his stock in his company and were taxed at 15 percent. In addition to crowing about his low tax rate, Buffett noted that he paid a lower rate than his secretary; as in, the woman who answers his phone. My guess is that she was not scraping by on $20,000 a year but was more likely making six figures like many Wall Street secretaries, which would explain her higher income-tax rate. But in the midst of a slow economic recovery—and heated political fighting between Democrats and Republicans—Buffett's admission was a gift to Democrats pushing for higher taxes on wealthy Americans. Here was a super-wealthy guy asking to be taxed more! President Barack Obama included a provision in his budget called the Buffett Rule, which aimed to ensure that the wealthiest paid a higher percentage of their income in taxes than middle-class Americans.

Buffett's op-ed made for great political theater, but it also confused nonwealthy people about taxes. The difference was not rich versus poor (though it may have been wealthy versus rich), but how people earned money—"source of income" in tax jargon. Everyone else at Berkshire Hathaway had a higher tax rate than Buffett, second on the *Forbes* rich list in 2011, because he or she was paid a salary, while Buffett owned a third of the outstanding shares of one of the most profitable investment companies of all time. Those shares, when sold, are taxed at a much lower rate than a high earner's salary. This distinction is the same for everyone, rich or poor, who earned a salary or sold shares. But the Buffett Rule had legs, and President

Obama proclaimed that wealthy people should pay at least as high of a percentage of their income in taxes as middle-class Americans, even though only about sixty thousand people—out of 145 million taxpayers—fell under this rule.

Surely it seemed unfair that a wealthy person paid such a low rate on high income. But lots of things about taxes are unfair, and they don't involve billionaires. The mortgage-interest deduction, which you can take if you own a home and itemize your taxes, applies to many more people, including me, and I think it's deeply unfair. If you're *not* a homeowner, you get nothing; if you are one, you get a break because you are no longer a renter, who some might argue needs a tax break more. As a homeowner in a town with high property costs, I'm thrilled that renters and people who have paid off their mortgages are subsidizing me, but I can't say I'd be as magnanimous if the situation were reversed. If you think taxation was meant to redistribute wealth from the rich to the poor, the mortgage deduction has done the opposite: it takes money that could be used for programs to help the poor and educate their children so they might have a better life—and one day buy a home—and subsidizes someone who makes enough money to own a home—or four, in the case of Carl, who has two mortgages solely for the deduction. Yet a 2011 poll by the *New York Times* and CBS News found that 90 percent of Americans thought homeownership was an important part of the American dream, and 45 percent of the people in that survey thought the federal government should do more to help the housing market. Yet only 25 percent of tax filers can take the mortgage-interest deduction—and most of them were rich, if not wealthy.

Second, people on the right side of the thin green line think about where their tax money goes and try to make decisions that minimize what they pay amid other factors. They have a choice as to where they live, and that can lower their taxes. The federal tax code may favor homeowners over renters. But if those wealthy homeowners live in high-cost-of-living states, the code favors their affluent counterparts in other parts of the country who need less to be rich and therefore are in a lower tax bracket. One solution for the overtaxed is to move to a state with no state income tax, such as Florida or Texas. Moving works great if you are a businessperson who doesn't need to live any place in particular and doesn't mind traveling. For everyone else the decision might not play out as cleanly. For starters, you would have to find the towns in those low-tax states with the lowest property taxes, then make sure you had a job there that pays just as well as the one you had in a high-tax city such as New York. Once you found that, you would reap the benefits. But that isn't as easy as I just wrote. Maybe you can't find the same type of job. Or the schools aren't as good. Or you don't like living in hot, humid central Florida in the summer. Therein lies the challenge. Areas with the greatest concentrations of people making a lot of money have those concentrations because wages are high and the taxes on those wages provide high-level services. The people who live there lose more of their income to taxes than they would elsewhere, but they get additional benefits, from good schools to professional fulfillment.

Third, people on the right side of the thin green line understand what taxes do to their income. All money we earn is taxed and retaxed and taxed some more. So much ire gets directed at the income tax, but let's consider an iPad. Say the list price for a basic one is $500, which it was in 2012. The real cost was much higher. First, you need to think what your income is. We each know what our employer pays us, but few calculate what we actually put in the bank. Take a salary of $52,000, or $1,000 a week. In Connecticut, if you were married and had your withholding set for a two-income family (so you would not owe taxes at the end of the year), you would take home $37,913.20 a year. That would include federal and state taxes and also withholdings for Medicare, Social Security, and unemployment compensation. That $500 iPad was not bought with pretax income, like contact lenses from a flexible spending account. It was bought with what was left after state and federal agencies took their share. While that $500 iPad would appear to cost you $531.75 at the cash register when Connecticut sales tax was applied, it really cost $729.32 out of your gross salary of $52,000. Or 37 percent more than the list price. This happens with everything you spend money on.

A wealthy person will use an accountant and a financial adviser to find the best ways to minimize taxes throughout the year, from saving for retirement to owning investments that don't incur a lot of tax in brokerage accounts and putting investments that are heavily taxed in tax-deferred accounts. The differences will be small year to year, but over decades they will add up. This type of planning works—far more effectively than trying to get paid in cash so you don't declare a few thousand bucks of income or stashing money in some obscure investment or offshore account that is hard to access and requires trusting people who are disreputable by choice of profession. While paying taxes is not fun, and paying taxes when you feel that you get nothing in return can be downright frustrating, there isn't an alternative.

Birkenfeld said he wanted me to focus not on him but on the man who oversaw all of private banking for UBS. This man was traveling the world drumming up business for the firm while sitting on philanthropic boards at home that burnished his reputation. When this executive was called before the Senate Permanent Subcommittee on Investigations, he lost all sophistication and spoke in halting English. As unbelievable as this guy was, Birkenfeld was equally unappealing. He had started to think of himself as a whistle-blower, a far more romantic title than *failed midlevel banker*. He cooperated with the federal government, but that was not enough to keep him out of prison. He ended up being sentenced for his complicity and did over three years in a federal penitentiary. But when he was released at the end of 2012, the US government paid him $104 million for services to his country. Under the federal whistle-blower laws, this amount was his cut of the back taxes and penalties his information had brought in from overseas accounts. He had become one of the greatest whistle-blowers in IRS history, and his supporters championed him as if he had revealed how a food company was poisoning babies. Ten months after receiving the money, Birkenfeld was arrested for driving while intoxicated in New Hampshire, which put his parole, if not his reward, in jeopardy.

I find the good that happened to Birkenfeld galling since he had been an eager participant in international tax evasion. Yet he showed the IRS how it was done, which the agency hadn't figured out on its own. Olenicoff, who kept Birkenfeld employed at UBS, also got him a lesser sentence and a reward from the federal government. Olenicoff himself ended up paying $52 million in back taxes and fines—a quarter of the account and seven times what he originally owed. Yet he avoided jail. I find the outcome unfair—one criminal was rewarded and the other was shown leniency—but it shows that even the richest people in the world cannot decide what taxes they pay. And if they can't, no one can. There are more important things that people can do with money—and that money can do for them.

SPEND IT

5

SPENDING TIPS FROM PEOPLE WHO SPEND A LOT BUT AREN'T BROKE

Paul Posluszny looked uncomfortable wedged into a high-backed leather chair in an office in lower Manhattan. It was too tight. He fidgeted. His massive arms and chest stretched the suit jacket that curled around his trunk-size neck. His face was young and fresh, like that of any guy in his early twenties, but his eyes were stoic. I couldn't help thinking that if he flexed, his suit would split apart the way David Banner's clothes did when he transformed into the Incredible Hulk. "I don't own a car," he told me. He had worked out a barter arrangement with a local Nissan dealership so he could drive an Armada. He also lived in a modest town house in Buffalo. His girlfriend was a teacher. He confessed that he was afraid to spend too much for fear he would go broke.

But Posluszny shouldn't have had any concerns. He had been a standout player at Penn State before the Buffalo Bills drafted him in

2007. His first contract paid him $4.75 million for four years, with $2.5 million of that guaranteed for just showing up. We were talking during the football lockout in 2011 when many players were worried about getting paid if the football season was canceled. But by all reports he was set to earn many millions more with his second contract. Still he was adamant that he did not want to be another player who spent all of his money and ended up broke. "It's the same old story," he told me. "There will be a handful of guys who will do the right things and they'll be set for life. Too many of us are taking out lines of credit, buying expensive homes and expensive cars. The next thing you know is, you're out of the NFL and you don't have a source of income. This is a very short period of time that you're playing." The average tenure in the league is less than four years—and three years are needed to qualify for the pension and health-care plan. He had played four seasons, so those concerns were behind him, but he couldn't be sure how the lockout would change the game and his ability to capitalize on his talent.

When it comes to spending, Posluszny is what I call a dissipator. A dissipator is a person who achieves his maximum wealth young—an athlete, an entrepreneur with a fluke idea, an inheritor—and will never have a chance to match it again. The two other types are accumulators, who amass a pile of money doing something that is intellectually interesting or challenging but wait until much later to spend it on something they are passionate about, and make-and-spenders, who see money flowing through their lives to fund what they want as they go along and make decisions on the fly. With spending, like debt, it should be simple to be on the right side of the thin green line whether you're a dissipator, an accumulator, or a make-and-spender. Beyond basic needs such as food and medical care, what we spend is totally within our control, unlike our investment returns or tax rates. Yet why does spending regularly derail people's plans despite the many examples that should give us pause? Because so little emphasis is put on the proper way to spend what we have for needs and wants.

Posluszny had received a lump sum. He was rich by any standard, but like all athletes he would have to manage his money carefully if he wanted to be wealthy when he was done playing football. Professional athletes are well-known dissipators—think Mike Tyson or Lenny Dykstra. But they are far from alone in struggling to manage what could be the high-water mark for their bank accounts. In the most recent Internet boom, employees at fast-growing companies that sold for enormous sums (social media companies such as Facebook and Twitter and all the smaller concerns looking to make money off our obsession with checking our iPhones and Galaxies) ended up with windfalls of ten or twenty times their annual salary just for being there at the right time. They are dissipators without the fear of a linebacker who knows the stories of players gone broke. Yet unlike football players, who know they are done at thirty, tech dissipators might believe they can do it again. They could spend aggressively on their lifestyle or invest in the hope of finding start-ups that will bring them another payout. The smartest ones realize that not only did they get lucky, but that they might not stay lucky or get lucky again. Mark Curtis, a financial adviser at Morgan Stanley in Palo Alto, California, the epicenter of lucky riches, told me that his smartest clients not only realize they are probably not going to have another windfall, but they put the money from their windfall in safe investments to make sure they can hold on to what has come their way. "In the nineties, those people who got the stock thought they'd do it again," he said. "Now the attitude is, 'I've hit a home run. Let's make sure I don't blow it with this money.'" Such a sentiment shows a concern not only with investment risk but also spending risk, which can erode wealth just as quickly.

Ron Carson, the founder of the Carson Wealth Management

Group in Omaha, Nebraska, who advises Posluszny and several other football players, focuses on clients' spending as much as investing. Over the years, he has come to think of football players as a lot like doctors: "They make a tremendous amount of money and save none of it," he told me. The difference is that doctors have a longer career. To help his clients understand what they need to do to balance spending and saving, Carson came up with a nifty initialism to get his point across: he calls it the RICH experience. Its letters highlight the adviser-client Relationship, the firm's ability to Inspire confidence, its dedication to Composing a financial plan, and, probably most important, Holding clients accountable. If clients spend way beyond what they have budgeted, no amount of investment returns can make up for that. "If it is a windfall, if it's unexpected, if it's something that you didn't plan for or prepare for, even if it's just a couple of million dollars, people think that's a lot and I can't run out of money," Carson told me. "Most of the time they expand their consumption and end up broke."

Carson has been ranked one of the top advisers in America by *Barron's* for several years, and he has grown rich on the steady fees of managing billions of dollars for clients. He believes he has the right advice to help clients succeed and achieve their goals, but he is willing to let people make their own decisions, even if they are destructive. (He tries to avoid the clients who will be hopeless no matter what he says. "If their first question is 'Can you arrange a loan against my first contract?' or they say, 'I have eleven brothers and sisters I want to support,' we shy away from them.") He prefers clients who plan for the unknown. Part of this was understanding the perils of lifestyle creep—the risk of spending money on things that have ongoing maintenance costs, such as homes, boats, club memberships. "It's stuff you accumulate like a snowball," Carson said. "As long as the cash flow is fine, it's okay. But when you have melting, it's tough."

When it comes to football players—and tech entrepreneurs who get lucky—what complicates matters further is just how young they are when they come into millions of dollars. People who have worked their entire lives to accumulate a sizable nest egg are often no better at spending it, but they have at least established a pattern to track what they're doing. "Remember what it was like when you were twenty-one years old," said Michael Conway, an adviser in New Jersey. "As a young man you think nothing is going to go wrong. But it does." Conway's goal with clients is to get them to think farther out. He advocates starting slowly, and not just for his athlete clients. "The biggest thing for all of us is delayed gratification. That would go for an executive, an athlete, or anyone. We buy into the hype that we need a bigger car, a bigger home. If you can concentrate on the long-term objectives, those things will fall into place."

Adam Carriker, another football player, learned this lesson in a costly way. Selected by the St. Louis Rams in the first round of the 2007 draft, he signed a five-year, $14.5 million contract with $9.5 million of that guaranteed. He promptly bought a big house in St. Louis and set about making a life there with his wife. He played a year for the Rams but missed the next season because of an injury. Then in his third season he showed up to practice one day and was told to see the coach. That afternoon he was on a plane across the country for Washington, where he had been traded. He ended up selling that house at a loss. "The best line I've heard was 'Don't live like a king for a little bit, live like a prince forever,'" he told me. "Once they've lived like a king, it's gone." Most of us don't have a $9.5 million cushion to soak up a mistake, but being princely has its advantages. That early loss, he said, changed his spending forever.

I'm not a great spender. I'm afraid to spend too much, and I hate having any consumer debt—credit cards, car loans. I should be spending money on plenty of things because I can afford to—nicer vacations, newer cars, a new weekend wardrobe that doesn't make me look like a college student at forty, or at least some casual shoes that aren't scuffed—but I won't. How I approach spending is no surprise to me. It's vexed me my entire life. I grew up buffeted by two horrible examples. When I was a child, my father was always well dressed, coiffed, and shaved. I don't remember seeing him with a tattered cuff or collar. He had one in every color, whatever the one was. When Ralph Lauren Polo shirts, with their horse and mallet-wielding man on the breast, became popular in the 1980s, he began buying them. I don't remember what they cost, but I do remember they were triple the price of a plain golf shirt. Soon they replaced his nonlogo shirts even though the old ones were still in excellent condition. He bought so many Ralph Lauren shirts at a time when we had so little that I came to hate everything with a polo pony on it. He had been living with his parents since getting divorced so his expenses were low, and perhaps they made him feel better about his postdivorce life. But I disdained those silly Polo shirts as a total waste of money so people could know what your shirt cost.

Later, when I was in college and just out, my mother's spending was what perplexed me. I noticed each time I went home to her condo more stuff in corners and on shelves. Little boxes and end tables began to crop up, none terribly expensive but none very useful either. I also noticed a lot of new jewelry—bracelets, charms, necklaces. They were nice but not any nicer than the pieces she already had. She had also taken on a couple of part-time jobs to supplement her income as a teacher, which wouldn't have bothered me—she had four months off a year—if she didn't complain so much about them. She was working extra jobs to pay for the things she wanted, but that work made her miserable. The disconnect was painful to watch.

Neither of my parents was rich, never mind wealthy. I felt they spent too much on things that ultimately didn't matter. They were make-and-spenders—representative of so many people who spend as much and more than they make. And spending the way they were wasn't something that ended well for a lot of people as they got older. Among retirees receiving Social Security, 53 percent of married couples and 74 percent of unmarried people depend on those benefits for half of their income, according to the Social Security Administration. A subset—23 percent of married couples and about 46 percent of single people—rely on Social Security for 90 percent of their income when the average monthly payment works out to about $14,400 a year.

When it came to my own spending, I considered my parents channel markers that I needed to navigate. The family member I looked to for financial guidance was Papa, my maternal grandfather. In retrospect, he was a better model for the big character traits such as honesty, morality, and humane directness. When it came to money, he would spend it to buy what he needed, but then he used what he bought until it fell apart. Shifts in fashion or obsolescence would not prompt him to replace something. I'm not much different. The shirts in my closet could be grouped by epoch, not color. I still hang on to three pairs of flannel trousers I bought at the Burberry store on Fifty-Seventh Street in Manhattan when Burberry was still known for its raincoats and sturdy Britishness. The trousers are out of style—unflattering pleats, cuffs that are too short—and about three inches too tight in the waist. But, still, they hang there. I justify keeping them because nothing is to be gained by getting rid of them: their absence would mean my wife's clothes would gain further ground in our closet. But in reality, their original price, paid almost twenty years ago, is what holds me back. I don't remember what I paid for them, but I remember that it seemed like a lot, to the point of being extravagant. That mentality is why every couple of years my wife forces me to throw out my rattiest clothes and buy replacements. At that point, a new epoch begins.

But I wouldn't call myself cheap. When I go out to dinner, I order what I want with the appropriate wine to match. I'll look at the prices, but they won't influence my decisions unless they're outrageous—aged filet mignon covered with foie gras and black truffles drenched in a thirty-year-old tawny port might trigger caution. The same goes for a vacation: we don't skimp; we enjoy ourselves. When I play golf, I go to a course fifteen minutes from my house that charges $195 for a round on a Sunday morning and not the one at the end of my street that costs $30. I can play in four hours at the more expensive course, whereas it would take me six hours, on a good day, at the one around the corner and it wouldn't be much fun. I pick and choose how I spend. I'm an accumulator—someone who gets more pleasure in not spending but will spend when necessary or justified. Our spending skews toward experiences or the highest-quality version of what we need, from clothes to cookware. I wouldn't turn down another bespoke suit, but I'd rather use that money to buy plane tickets for a vacation. You only need so much stuff, but you can never have enough stories.

Don Ross, who has plenty of stories, is an accumulator now spending money with gusto on a passion. He passes his days looking out over his property, which sits on a knoll in Napa Valley. He lives in a stone house built in 1921 on 2.5 acres of sloping vineyards—the smallest house, he said, he has ever lived in. With a view of Mount Saint Helena in the distance and rows of grape vines all around, he is living a life that is much different from the one he had in Louisville, Kentucky, where he sold shower doors. When we spoke, Ross was on his third wife and had finally found a great dog, Cooper. He said he couldn't be happier, having traded his business—which made him wealthy—for the less lucrative and more delicate craft of making wine. It didn't bother him in the slightest to spend money like water to make wine. "This wine business?" he said. "We don't make any money. I do it for love. I sell shower doors for money. To say we break even doesn't consider anything for my labor or my wife's labor."

Ross orders the bottles, labels, and the corks. He also stays on top of the agriculture, as he tries to buy all the chardonnay and pinot noir fruit that a couple of neighboring vineyards produce while tending to his own cabernet sauvignon grapes. It's labor-intensive; it also requires some luck. A spate of bad weather will render the wine unrecognizable and a total waste of money. But he isn't complaining: "In the shower-door business I feel like I do nothing." He was funding a fantastically expensive hobby with money from a lucrative business that bored him. He was wealthy enough to do pretty much whatever he wanted in life, but whether he could retain that freedom would be determined by how he managed his spending on his hobby.

Ross became a lover of wine in the 1980s and pursued that passion, particularly for Burgundy. He eventually acquired seven thousand bottles of wine in his cellar. A Californian by nature, he decided to buy a plot of land in Napa in 2003; it had cabernet sauvignon vines and cost him a fortune. He knows he paid too much for it, but the lifestyle of the wine country seduced him. He wanted to be part of the crowd of owners and producers, the sommeliers and wine consultants, all the people who make wine so romantic. "The people who love wine seem to really love wine," Ross said. "They're really smart, nice people. Our compensation is not a monetary one, it's a lifestyle one." The next year, he started Shibumi Knoll winery, choosing a Japanese word that means "effortless perfection." First it was cabernet. Then he found a great, old vineyard to buy chardonnay grapes from and later some pinot noir, to satiate his passion for Burgundy. He was doing what he had set out to do—make wine and not spend all the money he had made in the shower-door business.

In this, he was like many affluent people who have a desire for a new life from a hobby that makes no financial sense but completes them in a way their career did not. Owning a vineyard is high on that list for many accumulators. For others, it might be buying Thoroughbred racehorses, investing in a movie, being a partner in a restaurant, or, the ultimate childhood fantasy come true, owning a sports team. Ross had enough money to make his dream come true. He described his level of wealth as having everything he wanted except a private jet—though he said he had friends with jets.

How his expensive hobby became more than a vanity project was serendipity. In 2008, he took a couple of bottles of Shibumi Knoll chardonnay to a golf lesson. The pro passed the bottles on to his next student, a wine reviewer for *Wine Spectator*. In a blind tasting, that 2005 vintage received a rating of 97, making it one of the highest-rated chardonnays of all time. That's when the calls started coming in. "I never thought I wanted to be in the wine business because I thought a business should make sense," Ross told me. "I used to say the beauty of a hobby is a hobby doesn't have to make sense financially."

Ross got lucky, I figured. He was a mathematician by training whose first career had been working for NASA on the Apollo 12 program. That was the one after the moon landing. I could see how that would translate into shower doors, but what could he know about wine? But then I tasted it. All three selections were great, but the chardonnay—the vintage I drank from 2010 had received a 96 from *Wine Spectator*—was exceptional. My wife and I drank the whole bottle on a Sunday afternoon with some cheese while our children napped. The wine was silky and decadent. I told my wife something he had said in our conversation: "My wines are among the most served at the French Laundry." The French Laundry is the most famous restaurant in Napa wine country and one of the finest restaurants in the country. Saying his claim out loud sounded ridiculous: it was akin to his saying he had taught Derek Jeter how to turn a double play. So, I e-mailed the restaurant's sommelier, Dennis Kelly, to ask if what Ross had said was true. "Indeed," Kelly replied. "Shibumi Knoll is extremely popular with both our staff and our guests. The wines are very well made and offer fantastic value."

I was stunned. Ross wasn't delusional—and my palate wasn't as basic as I thought. He was instead a model for accumulators: not only was he not spending through all the money he had made earlier in life, but he was adding to his psychic wealth through winemaking. His life was better. His wine-country friends were more interesting. And he was receiving the kind of professional validation from the sommelier at the French Laundry that full-time winemakers dream about. Part of it, though, wasn't that Ross had millions of dollars to support his winemaking efforts, but that he and his wife were involved. He wasn't just cutting checks for others to do the work. He was there himself working at an age when his peers might have retired. In this, he had a direct knowledge of how his money was being spent. His wasn't profligate spending but reasonable spending after a life of accumulating.

The term *make-and-spend* sounds pejorative. It can be. But for some people who are wealthy it can also be a way of balancing income and outcome to achieve a goal—and a model mix of indulgence and restraint for everyone else. Stuart Sternberg is one of those people. He lives in Rye, New York, an affluent town about thirty minutes from Manhattan. He also owns the Tampa Bay Rays, a Major League Baseball franchise that is twelve hundred miles away. Sternberg, a man with an impish smile and a nest of black-and-white hair, made his fortune at Spear, Leeds & Kellogg, a trading firm that was acquired by Goldman Sachs in 2000. At the time, Spear, Leeds was the largest stock and options clearinghouse in the country. Sternberg's specialty was options trading, a sophisticated form of betting on what might happen to the price of an investment in the future, a perfect job for a savvy kid from Brooklyn who had a head for numbers. Then, in 2002, with hundreds of millions of dollars in his pocket, he retired. He was forty-three.

What he did next would be many boys' dream: he tried to buy a slice of his favorite baseball team, the New York Mets. Nelson Doubleday, of publishing and baseball renown, was looking to sell his half, and Sternberg expressed an interest in buying a share of it. Instead, Fred Wilpon, the other owner, bought out Doubleday. But as word got around Major League Baseball about Sternberg's interest, lots of owners approached him. Minority owners, even those with stakes of $20 million or more—such as the group of owners Wilpon had to find in 2012, when he lost millions in Bernie Madoff's Ponzi scheme—spend a lot of money for a seat in the owners' box, some sort of annual distribution, and no say in how the team is run. After looking into the Mets, Sternberg got smart quick about baseball spending. He passed on other teams and bought half of the Tampa Bay Devil Rays in 2004. Within a few years, he had acquired just about all of the team, which was then worth $145 million according to *Forbes*. What he got for his millions was the worst team in baseball and all the ongoing costs that came with it, from team payroll to stadium upkeep to the farm system and all the people who worked in all the offices of what he had just bought.

"I like things a bit messier," he told me over coffee at a bakery in the working-class town of Port Chester, New York.

Sternberg is fantastically rich, but he likes to be understated. I found it hard to pick him out among the tables of men eating breakfast at the bakery. He looked like any other suburban father, with graying hair and a plain button-down shirt. Had I seen his 7 Series BMW parked out front, it would not have been any easier: this is a BMW-centric part of the country, and not a single Rays marking was anywhere on the car. Married with four children, he rolled his eyes when I joked that he should have a vanity plate proclaiming his ownership of the team. That wasn't why he bought it. He was more interested in solving the team's problems, which in the beginning presented themselves the way options had in his previous career. "If given time and nothing else, those difficulties, mostly related to bad contracts, would diminish," he said. "Over time, like an option, they would expire."

Sternberg might sound like an accumulator: he had made his money and now he was spending it. But running a business such as a Major League Baseball team is different. It requires a keen sense of how to make and spend money; otherwise even his estimated $200 million fortune from the sale of Spear, Leeds would dissipate in a few years. He looked at spending differently. He believed in 2005 that he could turn the team around and bring baseball joy to Tampa Bay. He decided to spend on young players, not chase more expensive older players. His decision was not grounded in an old-school baseball hunch. He had just been a guy with season tickets to the Mets before he became an owner. Since he had never owned any professional team before, this conviction could have gone down as another bit of hubris from an ex–Goldman Sachs executive. But Sternberg figured the problem—more losses than wins—could be solved with financial knowledge.

To carry out his plan, he didn't try to hire some general manager who was an acolyte of Theo Epstein's, the wunderkind who engineered the Boston Red Sox's first World Series victory in eighty-six years. He went with a young banker at Goldman with an economics degree from Harvard and no discernible baseball ability. The man, Matt Silverman, had advised Sternberg on the purchase of the team, and he was now put in charge of sorting through the mess left by the previous owner. Silverman soon gained a reputation for being a smart spender. He knew the team did not have the deep pockets that the New York Yankees used to buy the best players on the market, nor the rabid fan base that filled Fenway Park and funded the Red Sox's acquisitions. Tropicana Field, where the Rays played home games, was last in the major leagues for attendance. Sternberg figured he could turn this around with some wins. If it cost him money at first, he consoled himself by saying he owned one of only thirty baseball franchises and that limited supply pretty much guaranteed he would get back what he paid for the team.

In 2008, a mere three years after he took control of the team, the Rays beat the Red Sox, who were the defending World Series champions, to go to the team's first World Series. They did so with an idiosyncratic manager in Joe Maddon and a roster of young players. Sternberg had spent wisely and taken his team further than it had ever gone before. But he didn't get the reward he had expected. Attendance—which is among the biggest variables of income for an owner—picked up, but it was nowhere near where it should have been for such a great team. He needed that increase for the make part of the make-and-spend strategy to work.

"Everyone at the time counseled me, 'Stu, you win some games, you're going to take off down there,'" he told me. "We believed it. But that second part hasn't happened. That was the one area that has been surprising."

Even though the team went to the World Series once and the play-offs three times from 2008 to 2012, its attendance never ranked higher than twenty-third out of the thirty major league ballparks. That was a marked improvement from last or second to last, but it was not what an owner of a great baseball team would expect. This mismatch between team success and fan attendance confounded

Sternberg's otherwise sound strategy of spending judiciously to make the team good. "We don't berate people for not showing up," he said. "It's easy, but it's wasteful, and it has no proper purpose. We can be pure and just focus on our success."

That's a nice, if not believable, sentiment. Sternberg was still plenty rich and getting richer as the value of the team increased—when we spoke, its price had tripled from what he had paid. But he still had to think about what he was spending. In 2012, he took the payroll up to $65 million, which does not sound like a lot by baseball standards, but it was a $25 million increase that had to come out of his pocket. "We said screw it," he said when I asked about the payroll. "We have signed up for losing anywhere from a good amount of money to a lot of money. This is all about winning this year, but this is the extent of what we can do. We could spend even more, but it would come at the expense of multiple years." (The increased spending did not help them win it all that year.)

Given his background, he said he was always looking at the revenue numbers and trying to make spending projections that would keep the team viable season after season. What he might not be making in revenues at the turnstile, he would make back whenever he sold the team. As he said, there are only thirty professional baseball teams, so their values will rise. He might be spending a lot of money, but he was also building wealth in his long-term investment as the value of the team rose. Sternberg had found a way to balance making and spending money on something he was learning about as he went along. It's what all of us who want to be on the right side of the thin green line have to do as we go through life.

Spending is spoken of too often in pathological terms—as a compulsion either to buy things we don't need or to hoard money in ways just as unhealthy. Tim Noonan is trying to change this. Noonan is in charge of capital markets insights at Russell Investments, a title that does little to explain what he does. His job is to work with financial advisers to help them do a better job with their clients. The hope for a firm like Russell, inventor of market indexes and purveyor of mutual funds, is that those advisers will buy Russell products for their clients. It's a soft sell. But Noonan's thinking is more expansive. Born in Detroit, Noonan looks like a tan, clean-shaven, better-dressed version of Robert Reich, the diminutive labor secretary under President Bill Clinton. He answers questions in looping digressions, punctuated by bits of jargon. But since the Great Recession, he has been working on a way to get people to spend their money better when they retire. He calls it "decumulating safely." "Many make the mistake that money is the most important thing, but what if it is time?" he asked me during a visit from Seattle. "How much time do I need to keep doing something to get to a level of security to keep my promises?" The typical advice for someone who has stopped working is to spend 4 percent of his or her savings per year. But that only works if the person has saved many millions of dollars and is older. "It's inaccurate," he said. "If you consider increased tax rates and interest rates, it depends on your age. If you're forty, have ten million dollars, and you think you're done, you say, 'I want to spend four hundred thousand dollars a year.' But you're too young to do that. But if I'm eighty, I should probably take nine percent a year." This is based on practical thinking as well as historical precedent: most people cannot imagine their lives more than ten years in the future and a forty-year-old is going to live through many more market cycles that could impact his wealth and ability to spend than an eighty-year-old. Noonan wants people to think instead about their "funded status," a jargony way to talk about whether they can spend what they want now and when they stop working. It requires them to get to a certain amount of savings for sure, but it also depends on their being able to stick to a plan—don't call it a budget—and adjust if they have to. That amount of money will pay for what he calls promises, and I would call wealth. Those promises could be walking in the woods with your dog, paying for things for children and friends, or traveling around the world. He believes most people should be 125 to 135 percent funded. And he wants them to evaluate it often to make sure the plan still holds true.

"The best strategy is to be more restrained in the early years to get more options later on," Noonan said. "What I'm trying to do is navigate the trade off of how much time I'm going to continue to work versus how much time I have left. The closer you get to death, your withdrawals go up."

But most people do not want to step back and have that conversation in the middle of their lives, let alone at the end. They are trying to decide how to manage their consumption while they're in the make-and-spend mode, not when they're dissipating it or acting as pure accumulators. In this, someone such as Posluszny is quite rare, among all young wealthy people and not just football players. Noonan says the conversation has to be about the balance between consumption, what you need now, and bequest, what you need in the future. One requires impulse control; the other demands an imagining of a distant time most people cannot comprehend.

This takes me to a different kind of football player, ones who played in the low-wage era of the 1970s. For one, all the players from the 1970s knew they would have to work after football, whether or not they spent all the money they made. They were having a run of good luck, the way many people do in their careers. But they knew that streak was going to end. They intuitively knew what Mark Rank would empirically determine decades later: their income was going to drop and probably wouldn't bounce back. They spent accordingly.

Today, someone like Ed Marinaro would be flush with cash to

spend as soon as he left college. When he was drafted in 1972, he never expected to become rich for life. "Back then no one was talking about what they made," he said. "We all knew we were going to have to get jobs when our careers were over. A lot of guys worked to create relationships for when they were done, unlike the guys today. We knew that when we left the game, our two greatest assets were, we were going to have a few extra bucks and our reputational goodwill was going to carry us the rest of our lives." In his day Marinaro was great. "I broke the Cornell single-game rushing record in my second game," he told me. "I broke the Ivy League record in my fourth game. I broke the Cornell single-season record in my sixth game." He was the first college running back to run for more than four thousand yards, and he broke more than a dozen NCAA records. He was a runner-up for the Heisman Trophy his senior year, and that led to his being drafted in the second round by the Minnesota Vikings. He received a three-year contract for $100,000, with $25,000 of that guaranteed as a signing bonus. He promptly took $10,000 from that check and spent it on a purple Porsche—the Vikings team color. ("It took a lot of balls to pull into training camp as a rookie in that car when I hadn't even made the team," he said. "All the other guys were driving station wagons.") He played for the Vikings for four years, appearing in consecutive Super Bowls, before joining the New York Jets, where Joe Namath was the quarterback. He ended his six-year NFL career with the Seattle Seahawks. This journeyman's career for a college standout is not uncommon in professional football, where college greats struggle for success. But it came after a meteoric rise. "I went from obscurity to *Sports Illustrated*," he told me. "What do you do in your life to prepare you for that instant of fame? It was overwhelming." Fortunately, he was fairly grounded—his father owned a sign-painting business—and that gave him perspective on what he was earning and spending.

Something else helped more. When he joined the Jets, he went to Los Angeles with Namath in the off-season and was asked to do a screen test to replace Lee Majors in *The Six Million Dollar Man.* The pay was $10,000 an episode or $220,000 for the season. His last contract with the Vikings, after four seasons and two Super Bowls, was for $25,200. He didn't get the role, but it got him thinking. It was a lot more money than he could make in football or with his Cornell degree. At twenty-eight, when his career was done, he went to Hollywood to try acting. He gave himself two years, which he had the savings to cover, and he figured that if it didn't work out, he would go into the hotel business. He started getting parts immediately, and before his two-year window was up, he landed a recurring role on the comedy *Laverne & Shirley.* The next year, he started on *Hill Street Blues,* the era-defining police drama, which would run for seven seasons. While his acting career petered out by the late 1990s, he had had a solid television career.

When it came to spending money, neither professional football nor Hollywood swayed him. Marinaro planned a bit, but mostly he didn't spend aggressively in case his good fortune ended. "There were 139 guys who went out for the freshman football team," he told me. "I remember saying, 'I want to make the team.' I was always just planning far enough ahead so I didn't dwell on things." He carried that into the pros. "After practice as a rookie, I wasn't saying I can always get a job in the hotel business. I allowed myself the freedom not to worry so much. I just took care of the task at hand." But more than that, he controlled the other side of the ledger, his spending. His earnings were always going to fluctuate, so he learned early on to save and to spend on a select number of things. Or as he put it, he knew what was important to him and what wasn't. Cars and clothes didn't matter—he's driven the same GMC Yukon for nearly twenty years—but fishing and golf trips, good food and wine, did matter. Beyond that, he sought out advice and listened to it. He relied on a Cornell alum who worked as a money manager to advise him on investing. Marinaro said he kept one thing in mind that served him well: "I was famous, but I wasn't rich, and I knew it." While the purple Porsche may seem to have been an extravagant use of his signing bonus, his apartment rent at the time was $180 a month, and he shopped for his own groceries after practice. As we talked, I forgot I was speaking to someone who was once so famous: he seemed like any other sixty-something guy becoming aware of his mortality and worried about cutting his expenses.

Roger Staubach, the Heisman Trophy–winning quarterback and Dallas Cowboy star, had restraint when it came to spending for different reasons. He had played for the Naval Academy in a way and at a time not dissimilar to Marinaro's at Cornell: Staubach was a great football player when being a great football player at a service academy—or Ivy League school—did not seem odd. In 1963, as quarterback for Navy, he won the Heisman Trophy as a junior, a pass to fame and wealth. Instead, when he graduated the next year, he joined the other midshipmen to serve his four years in the Navy, including a tour of duty in Vietnam. After he had fulfilled his obligation, he joined the Dallas Cowboys, which had drafted him in the lowly tenth round out of college. He didn't start for three seasons. But in 1971 he took over and the next year led the Cowboys to victory in Super Bowl VI. He played in three more Super Bowls, ending his career after winning Super Bowl XII in 1979. He also played in six Pro Bowls and was inducted into the NFL Hall of Fame five years after he retired. For this illustrious career he has gone down in football history as the greatest quarterback of the 1970s.

But off the field, Staubach told me he had a different life, one where wealth was not assured and spending was tight. While in the Navy, he got married and had three children; he and his wife would have two more while he was playing football. He may have been a Heisman Trophy winner and a member of America's Team, as the Dallas Cowboys were known, but at the outset of his professional career, six years after winning the Heisman, he was a father of three with bills to pay. "They didn't pay quarterbacks quite what they do today," Staubach told me in his soft, clear voice. "That was a bit of an issue." Staubach, with a degree in engineering, found work in the off-season to pay the bills. After interviewing with several companies, he took a job working for the Henry Miller Group, an insurance and real estate firm in Dallas. He was assigned to sell key-man insurance, the kind of coverage companies buy to protect themselves in case an essential employee can no longer contribute to the business. It was perfect for someone who himself was the key man of the game. "My life changed when I went and started working for Mr. Miller," Staubach said. "It all started because I had three kids to worry about and a wife."

That selling insurance was a life-changing event for a Heisman Trophy winner and one of the most successful and best-known quarterbacks of the 1970s seems odd today. But he knew he was going to need a career when football ended. "During the off-season, I worked out and I worked in the company," he said. "I decided I wanted to continue to build a real estate service company in the off-season." He did that, and after three decades he sold the company for over $600 million. While he certainly had connections from an illustrious football career, most players have the same access and not much comes of it. Staubach was more industrious. "Besides football and being with my family," he said, "I didn't do anything else besides work."

But he also had an innate sense of how to spend the money he had. When he started his own firm, he realized that it cost a lot to maintain various offices, and he paid close attention to where his money was going. "I'd get these expense reports and they were for real," he said of the Staubach Company in the 1980s. "It became very worrisome to have all the financial responsibility. We had six or seven offices at that time." So he kept his business spending in check just as he did his personal spending.

As we were talking, he remembered one of the Reef Points that was drilled into him at the Naval Academy. These absurdist rhymes are hard to memorize but constitute some of the shared knowledge of any midshipman. "How's the cow? Sir, she walks, she talks, she's full of chalk. The lacteal fluid extracted from the female of the bovine species is highly prolific to the . . . and then you say the number of glasses on the table," he told me, reciting it five decades later as if he were still a plebe. "You got all these stupid things to memorize, but it's discipline. I didn't think it was very important. I thought I was doing the important things. It took me a while but I memorized them."

At first, when he began reciting this, I figured our conversation bored him. But I realized that so much of his success in life was a function of the kind of discipline that forced him to memorize something so odd. The area where the spending line between being wealthy and rich is starkest is in such discipline. "It was a real balance of what you take out of life and what you give back," Staubach told me. Striking that balance is key for everyone.

A little over a year after my first conversation with Posluszny, I phoned him to check in. He was living in Jacksonville, Florida, where he had been traded to the Jacksonville Jaguars. His fiancée, whom he had dated since college, had just finished a master's degree in education. She was looking for a job as a teacher. They were planning a simple wedding ceremony in Butler, Pennsylvania, his hometown. Toward the end of our call, the conversation turned again to cars. I asked him what he was driving these days. He laughed and said he had been forced to give up the Nissan Armada when he had to leave Buffalo and hadn't found another gig doing promotions in exchange for a car. So he bought a Chevy Tahoe. Then he laughed, as he recalled something else we had discussed. "I was talking about getting a BMW," he said. "When it was time to pull the trigger, I got nervous. An eighty-thousand-dollar car was too much. So I downsized." What did he get instead? "I bought an Audi. It's still that good German engineering, but it was a little less expensive."

Saving $10,000 on a German luxury car is not skimping. But it shows Posluszny's attention to spending. It's all the more remarkable because his second contract, the one that had brought him to Jacksonville, was worth $42 million with $15 million of it guaranteed. He signed it in July 2011, three months before his twenty-seventh birthday, and yet he was still cautious about spending. When his first contract is factored in—$4.75 million with $2.5 million guaranteed— he will have made no less than $17.5 million, but will ultimately make something between that and the nearly $47 million in the contracts' headline numbers. (NFL contracts are all written with performance bonuses, some easy to attain, some farcical. It is the guarantee that matters.) Let's say he makes a minimum of $20 million. At least $2 million will go to his agent, and another $8 million, for simplicity's sake, will go to pay taxes. That means, at the very least, he has $10 million in his brokerage account, earning 5 percent, or $500,000, a year. By Noonan's calculations that is not enough for him to be drawing $500,000 a year from age thirty-two onward, though from my conversations with Posluszny his promises to himself and others seemed fairly modest. His wife, after all, was teaching even though her husband was a famous NFL player. A financial psychologist like Brad Klontz might say that Posluszny's buying the less expensive Audi and not the BMW he wanted was an example of a flawed money script: neither car would impact his lifestyle so he should buy the one he wanted. Still, how many other people in his situation would hesitate before buying an $80,000 BMW because it cost too much?

Posluszny is an excellent NFL lineman and a wealthy young man. What is exceptional is his thinking about spending. His father was a car mechanic and his mother a teacher; he went to Penn State on a football scholarship. While he did well academically, it's certain that without football he would be earning a lot less. He knew that the vast amount of money he was making now would be the bulk of his lifetime earnings. He would be dissipating his wealth as soon as he retired, probably in his early thirties—forcing him into a way of thinking about spending that most people don't have to consider until they hit their sixties. He was being conservative, more so than most people who earn a similar amount over decades of working, because he needed to preserve money. When it comes to spending, whether from a windfall or steady earnings, few people think like Paul Posluszny— which means the bottom lines of BMW, Audi, and all their competitors are safe, and most people will spend themselves onto the wrong side of the thin green line.

6

THE EDUCATION RACE: WHERE THE WEALTHY SPEND AND WHY IT MATTERS

Driving through Middlebury, Connecticut, in search of the Westover School, I was taken back to my own time at prep school in Wilbraham, Massachusetts. The two towns were similar: small, quaint, but worn, with the schools like a jewel preserved from another era. In the case of Middlebury, it was a hundred-year-old girls' school that had educated Rockefellers and Astors. Alice Tully, an heir to the Corning Glass fortune and the namesake for the main concert hall at the Juilliard School, had been a student, and so, too, had the inspiration for Daisy Buchanan in F. Scott Fitzgerald's *The Great Gatsby*. As I rounded a corner and drove up a slight hill, I saw an unmistakable sight: the perfectly maintained buildings and grounds of a classic boarding school. Founded in 1909, Westover looked from the road pretty much the same as I imagined it had always looked. All the buildings were painted a shade of yellow that I'd call Dijon mustard but that one administrator claimed Benjamin Moore had mixed just for them. The shutters were deep green, a hunter green, though the color may have had a fancier name. The main building—built around a sheltered, quiet square—was designed by Theodate Pope Riddle, one of the first female architects in America. The paths were only wide enough for walking, but they felt quaint, not cramped. One of the guides made a point of showing me a small chapel that was clearly a point of pride.

Today Westover is less interested in being a finishing school for well-born girls than producing young women who get into top colleges and go on to make their own way in the world. Its headmistress, Ann Pollina, was a former mathematics and calculus teacher who had led the school for fifteen years when we met. She was not a firebrand but a reformer, looking to modernize the ethos of an old institution. I had come to sit in on one of the school's enrichment classes. Sponsored by a nonprofit called Invest in Girls, the class was meant to teach schoolgirls financial skills. Unlike similar programs aimed at teaching money skills, this class aimed to prepare girls for finance jobs later in life. Programs like these—targeted, specific, enriching, and unique—are a selling point for private schools. They feed into what parents crave—a way to give their children extra benefits in life that doesn't seem as unfair as using their influence to get them into college or calling in a favor for their first job. "We wanted to help them understand what women do in business," Pollina told me. "We wanted to help them get a picture of what women in those fields *really* do." She was equally proud of the school's other innovations, such as Women in Science and Engineering, or WISE, and another program that uses technology to link up schools to share their different academic specialties. Parents and children, locked in the college race, sought advantages like these that they felt private schools could deliver to them better than even the best public schools. While no private school would say this guarantees admission to a top college, if not an Ivy League school, that is the hope of the high achievers these schools attract.

In the classroom at Westover, I was taken by the girls' inquisitiveness and willingness to ask all types of questions. No one seemed at all shy or afraid to be called out, at least in the class. They were there to figure out something on their own that they felt they should learn or had failed to grasp from their parents. "My mom always wanted to teach me about finances," Cailee Tallon, who had had a bank account since she was eight and wanted to be a doctor, told me after the class ended. "When this program was offered, I really wanted to be part of it. I don't want to be in a position when I graduate college that I don't know how to handle my money." Gabby DeBartolomeo gave a more kidlike answer: "I decided to sign up for it because my mom is in marketing and my dad sells stuff for Verizon. I never understood what they did." Yet she did understand that the internships offered in conjunction with the program could expand her sense of possible careers. "I think I want to be a doctor, but I don't want to be that person who looks back in twenty years and wishes she had become a lawyer or a businessperson." Responses like these, candid, unvarnished, as only sixteen- and seventeen-year-olds could be, were ostensibly about the program. But to me they also showed a mature, curious group of students exploring a subject—finance—that many adults do not grasp. How many other high school juniors were already worried about regrets that don't hit most people until they are triple their age? To others, these offerings might speak to the tremendous advantages that private schools give their students, advantages to see their life differently that other kids don't have. An opportunity like this may be one of the great benefits of a private boarding school, or it may be indicative of the widening educational divide between those with financial resources and those without. Such wisdom does not come cheap.

Westover costs $47,000 a year for tuition, room, and board, more than many second-tier colleges. Committing to paying essentially another college tuition before college represents a whole different level of spending, but the mentality of the people who are willing to pay that kind of money on private education at all the levels before boarding school presents challenges to knowing who is on the right side of the thin green line. It's not as easy as saying it's the people who pay for private school versus those who do not when they could.

My appreciation of private education is biased. I feel that I owe so much in my life to my four years at Wilbraham & Monson Academy, a good but not top-ranked private school. Its teachers along with the environment and ethos put me on a path to a better life than I had ever imagined. Before going to the Academy, I was living in a desperate, occasionally violent lower-income neighborhood. I had gained a lot of weight and had few friends, at least none that I would seek out today. I was probably depressed. But the Academy showed me something better. It wasn't hard to do that. The teachers at my middle school in Ludlow, Massachusetts, were comically inept, like characters created for a campaign against teachers' unions except that they were real. I'll never forget my first day of social studies class in seventh grade with a teacher who wanted to be called Mr. T. Obese and immobile, he spent a good part of that class showing us the proper way to open a textbook so the spine would not break. While I can't recall any of the many films he showed us that year, I can still see him snoring in waves and warbles at his desk. At Wilbraham & Monson, it was as if my academic life had gone from *Police Academy* to *Dead Poets Society*. I am forever grateful to the financial-aid officers who made it possible for me to attend and allowed me to compete against—and outperform—far richer students.

With my own daughters, I would never wait until ninth grade to expose them to the world that Wilbraham & Monson opened for me. My older daughter started at a Montessori school when she was two, a half-day program five days a week. Initially I thought this, my wife's idea, was ridiculous—not to mention a waste of $24,000 a year. But then I saw what it did for her, how it made her so much more comfortable in new settings, guided her curiosity and channeled her energies while also teaching her the patience to sit at circle time for thirty minutes by the end of the year. These sound like small things, but they are quite an accomplishment for any two-year-old. We left that school after two years because the good things they taught were offset by the demands made by minor royalty and major hedge-fund managers. The socioeconomic hierarchy ran the gamut from upper-middle-class to generationally wealthy, which we did not consider the most realistic environment for our daughter to develop in. But we found another independent school for her and our younger daughter that meshed better with our values. I came away convinced that all of those annoying, impossible-to-like Manhattan parents who compete to get their children into the best nursery schools were onto something—even if their motivations were all wrong. The research on the value of early-childhood education is on their side. Yet even among the rich, the focus is still on high school and college, when any incremental gains will require a lot more spending. The parents on the right side of the thin green line are the ones who realize that spending money early on their children's education is going to have a greater impact on their lives and set them up best later on.

Let's take a look at what seem to be the three strains of thinking on money and education: the disbelievers, the privileged sons, and the nursery obsessives. The breakdown is not the only determinant of what might happen in their children's lives. A disbeliever's child could become a wildly successful entrepreneur, while a privileged son could have a sterling academic pedigree but little ambition or ability to do for himself. Those of us in the nursery-obsessive camp may have children who are perfectly content in the middle of the pack (well, let's hope for the upper middle, at least).

Susan Beacham is a disbeliever. While she does not see spending money on test prep to get kids into college as entirely useless, she believes in a more important opportunity: to teach kids how to make money on their own. Her view, which she has imparted on two college-aged daughters, is born of her own hardscrabble beginnings. She grew up working-class Irish on the gritty South Side of Chicago in the 1960s and 1970s, where she was far from being a star student. She hadn't even thought of college until she was taking the bus to the Loop shortly after finishing high school and saw her sixth-grade teacher. "She said, 'Why aren't you in college?'" Beacham recalled. "I told her, 'I'm going to work.'" The teacher convinced her that she needed to continue her education, something her parents hadn't discouraged but certainly had not pushed. Her father worked as a sales manager for Sears Roebuck, her mother stayed home, her older sister was already married and raising a family. They were blue-collar, and their lives had turned out fine within that enclave. But Beacham decided to go to what was then called weekend college—Friday, Saturday, and Sunday. ("I did that in three years," she told me. "There is nothing more motivating than when you're paying your own bills.") When she finished, she went into banking. She had wanted to work at Continental Illinois Bank, then the most prestigious name in the city before it became the biggest bank failure in America. They wouldn't hire her so she went to Northern Trust, which offered her a job in the back office. She took it, even though she still makes the point decades later that the back office was where the bank put people from the South Side, the implication being it was a lesser role and carried with it less opportunity. Her future husband was working several floors above her in the trust department because he came from an affluent Chicago suburb—at least that was why she believed he got the better assignment.

After a few years, Beacham left, having decided she wanted to go to law school. Only she couldn't get into one. Family lore has it that her father called the pope to get her into Loyola Law School, but that's not plausible. Why would the pontiff take her father's call? It was more likely he talked to a local priest who reached out to a Jesuit friend who got her admitted. She said her father insisted that she get in because he had paid for Catholic school her whole life and a Catholic law school should accept her. Alas, this isn't a story of her proving everyone wrong. Those admissions officers were right in turning her down. She graduated and got a job working in the state's attorney office when Richard M. Daley was in charge of it. But after she failed the bar exam the third time, she said Daley brought her into his office and asked if she was trying to beat his record. It took him three tries to pass. She demolished his record, failing seven times before the test administrators suggested she quit wasting her money and their time. She took their advice and returned to banking, which turned out to be a good fit. "I went back to Northern Trust and I met my husband and I got married," she said.

After a stint on the West Coast for Wells Fargo bank, where she worked with really wealthy families such as the Gettys, she returned to Chicago, where she and her husband settled in an affluent suburb to raise their two girls. But she grew tired of banking. In 1999 she was working at Bank of America and took a buyout when NationsBank bought it. She started her own company bent on educating children about money. It all centered on a pig. Not any swine, but a money-savvy piggy bank, with separate slots marked *spend, save, donate,* and *invest*. This clever idea was inspired by the widows and divorcées she saw come into Wells Fargo and Bank of America with no clue about money. She said they were as ignorant about it as children. "I thought if my daughter was learning Latin, how can she not learn about the four choices of money?" Beacham said. "I decided my girls were not going to learn about money at a point of crisis." The piggy bank was a stroke of genius and helped her separate from the crowd of people who profess knowledge about kids and money. It has made her quite successful—probably more so than if she had passed the bar exam.

Yet she told her kids from the outset that she would limit how much she would pay for their education—a sentiment akin to blasphemy in the richest towns in America. Her girls went to public school in affluent Lake Bluff, and they had academic tutors like all the other kids. But she was not going to write a blank check for college. "They each get forty thousand dollars a year for four years," she said. "We've been talking about this since freshman year of high school. My kids get it. These are enlightened kids, not entitled kids." She selected the number because that was how much her husband's alma mater, Denison University, cost at the time.

Forty thousand dollars a year is not cheap, but it is less than a boarding school such as Westover and most top universities (which is pretty outrageous, since tuition increases make mediocre private colleges seem like a bargain at $35,000 a year). She had been a private banker and her husband had made equally good money as a consultant, so they would, I'd have guessed, preach education at all costs. But whether through genuine conviction in the value of money or some lingering insecurity about her own educational route, Beacham stood firm—even when one daughter pleaded to go to her dream school, New York University. Beacham told her she could go to the University of South Carolina, which is $20,000 less per year. Nor would she let her daughter borrow the additional $20,000 per year. Her rationale was the daughter would likely go into public service and not earn enough to pay off the debt. That she might learn more, choose to study something else, or make better connections at a more prestigious school didn't factor into Beacham's decision.

"They're hardworking and they understand that," she said. "Our world is not just where we go to school. It's our community. And I'd argue that the people who can connect the dots for you are everywhere."

A study published in 2012 in the *Journal of Political Economy* found that the success of a child was not related so much to a father's income as to the father's intelligence. In the paper, "Rich Dad, Smart Dad: Decomposing the Intergenerational Transmission of Income," the authors wrote that a father's income and his child's success had been linked, but without evidence on how that was transmitted. Their research showed that the mechanism, as they called it, for transferring success from father to child was not money but educational level. Someone who became rich in a way that could be equated with luck more than skill had less chance of passing on success to his children. The opposite was true for a father whose success was based on his intelligence: there was wealth in that. If you have ever spent any time in a private school in America, you would not be surprised by this finding: the parents with the most money may be wise and serious people whose wealth is a consequence of strong leadership qualities that made them successful, or they may be horrible buffoons whose riches came to them in a windfall, have become their identity, and can offer little more than new buildings to a school. (The school my older daughter first attended had a wing named after a wealthy family in town that was nationally known because of a murder committed by one of its scions.) Either way, it is not their money that will determine if their children have the resilience to make it through life.

Still, I found Beacham's view of education jarring. It was hard for me not to see it as resentment based on her educational background. She had surely been at a credentials disadvantage in the credentials-heavy world of private banking. But I knew my reaction said as much about me as her. She probably had a more rational, realistic view of college than I or most people I know do. Plenty of Ivy League graduates amount to less than they should, while lots of entrepreneurs passed through little-known colleges on their way to great success. She gives voice to people whose children can't get into the top schools or who didn't save enough along the way to send them where they wanted to go. It's a modified form of saying "Why would I want that?" when that thing is what you truly want. Yet I am in the camp that says spending on my daughters' educations is a good thing that will give them the best chance at doing what they want in life when they will be competing against kids from around the world, not just their neighborhood. My opinion is linked to my belief that education freed me from poverty and gave me a much better life than I could otherwise have imagined. For Beacham, education had not been as clearly important. Her success was more the result of innate pluck and perseverance. Her father never took a day off from work and arrived on time even after a crippling Chicago snowstorm. Her grandmother, who lived with them, talked to her about the cost of things, driving around the neighborhood pointing out the values of different homes. From Beacham's telling, these were industrious family people who sat on their stoops and gossiped about each other but still ran over to fix something for the person they had just maligned. She wanted her daughters to be successful, but she wanted them to work for it as she had.

"People in a high-net-worth community think digging drains in Brazil will look good on a college application and develop their kids' character in some ways," Beacham said. "These families have a hard time making their kids work. They think there is something more competitive that we need to do. We need to be teaching these kids to put work skills in their toolbox."

Instead, those hours are filled with tutoring—on top of sports, community service, and various extracurricular activities. In the year after the Great Recession started, Steve Pines, executive director of the Education Industry Association, told me that spending on tutoring had increased 5 percent, down from 8 to 10 percent growth in the boom years. That it was still growing showed just how essential tutoring has become. Even if their children are not slipping behind, parents will spend money on tutors so they can get further ahead. Sandy Bass, editor and publisher of *Private School Insider*, an online newsletter aimed at the anxious Manhattan set, said that most parents have unrealistic expectations from tutoring. "You're not going to go from a 550 to an 800 on the SAT, but you can count on a hundred-point rise," she told me. "A lot of that is just getting a kid used to taking the test." With a 550 as the base, that would be a 20 percent increase in a kid's score, which is nothing to sniff at. My concern, though, is parents don't think about the costs beyond the tutoring fees, namely what this kind of constant focus on certain measures does to students when they become adults. "Not only does it jeopardize your child's 'studenthood'—those qualities that make learning happen," said Lloyd Thacker, a former college admissions officer and the executive director of the Education Conservancy. "But someone finding your way for you and packaging you in the process jeopardizes your ability to be yourself." But most people, poor, rich, or wealthy, cannot get out of their own way.

Shamus Khan is from the second strain of thinking about spending on education, the privileged-sons approach. He has made it his career to dissect and understand the motivations of this elite class. His father was an accomplished surgeon in Boston, and that success bought Khan one of the best secondary-school educations in America, four years at the über-elite St. Paul's School in New Hampshire. An experience such as this is formative. All of the St. Paul's graduates I have met over the years seem to have closer ties with their prep-school friends than anyone else before or after those years. Khan used his experience and a subsequent stint teaching at the school to write *Privilege: The Making of an Adolescent Elite at St. Paul's School*—a book that he called a "cultural study of inequality." I thought of it more as an anthropologist's journey among a strange and privileged tribe of boys and girls at a place that outsiders might find hard to comprehend. Khan was as wealthy as many of his classmates, but he has brown skin. That meant when he arrived on campus in 1993, he lived in the "minority students dorm," which was filled with financial-aid students from inner-city neighborhoods who had nothing in common with Khan beyond their nonwhite skin. Khan's parents were both immigrants: his father from Pakistan and his mother from Ireland. They were thrilled that they could give Khan and his brother private-school educations, but Khan said he struggled with the easy access St. Paul's provided to the top colleges in America. The school doesn't send one or two kids to the Ivy League each year or maybe every other year; it sends scores annually. He said he visited Harvard University his junior year, and after staying with a St. Paul's friend whose only friends seemed to be other boarding-school students, he decided to find some place where no St. Paul's students went. He chose Haverford College, a small liberal arts college in Pennsylvania (though he now teaches at Columbia University). Most parents and students would see this decision as foolish: If you could get into Harvard, why wouldn't you go? He said his choice stemmed from his desire to get away from the insular world of purchased privilege he had experienced.

Today, as a sociologist, his focus is not on the poor but on the rich. He has much to say about how inequality—and the decreasing rate of economic mobility—relates to parents' spending on education. One of the things he looks at is how eager rich and wealthy parents are to spend vast sums of money on their children. "Think of your kid as a good," he told me. "The more you put into it, the more you expect to get out of it." These investments are not all academic. He mentioned a common expense, sports, which are good for a child's physical well-being and teach lessons about teamwork, winning, and losing. Excelling in sports is also a good way to get into a better college than you might have otherwise. Another expense is money spent on cultural opportunities—from seeing plays, musicals, dance recitals, and opera to visiting museums and foreign countries. He admits that this enriches children, but it also gives them the ability to recognize moments that less privileged children will miss.

"The amount upper-middle-class people invest in their child's education is astonishing," he said. "What surprises me is how expensive it is to get those payoffs. And it's not guaranteed. When you think about that cost, the return rate seems kind of low."

This idea sent me to do my own calculation about how much it would cost to send one of my daughters through private school in Fairfield County and then four years of college. It was staggering. Private school for fifteen years—including two years of Montessori and one of prekindergarten—would be $508,000, at current prices. Four years at my alma mater would cost $230,000. To educate one child privately for her whole life would cost nearly three-quarters of a million dollars, all of which is after income taxes are taken out and doesn't account for inflation. And I have two kids. When I told Khan about my back-of-the-envelope calculation, he thought I had lowballed the number. He pointed out that I hadn't factored in the annual shakedown from the development office at all of these schools and the cost of any tutors and coaches we might hire along the way.

While my wife and I might be able to get away with writing a four-figure check to our daughters' schools, wealthier families are expected to think five and six figures, maybe even a wing of a building. Even after spending all that money, Khan said he calculated that a child only has a 75 percent chance of staying at the same economic level as his or her parents.

Khan is mining a robust vein. Sean F. Reardon, a sociologist at Stanford University, found in his research a 30 to 40 percent difference in academic performance based on family income between children born in 1976 and those born in 2001. He found that what he calls the "income-achievement gap" is twice as large for families in the 10th and 90th income percentiles as the racial-achievement gap between black and white students. "Fifty years ago, in contrast, the black-white gap was one and a half to two times as large as the income gap," he wrote. That is promising in many ways. It shows that wealthy black children have similar levels of achievement to wealthy white children. But it is also distressing since it threatens to undermine the myth of America, that a child can rise from poverty to wealth, or at least to a better occupation than his or her parents. Reardon wrote the difference came not from something intrinsic in the wealth of the parents but from their ability to spend money on their children's education. We may have greater racial and ethnic diversity at the top of American society, but if what Reardon found continues, we will have little economic diversity: a multicultural plutocracy is still a plutocracy.

Khan sees schools such as St. Paul's as perpetuating and even increasing inequality in America, but he also understands why parents will spend so much to give their child a chance. "As inequality increases, falling from the one-tenth of one percent to the one percent is really a big fall because wealthier people have gotten wealthier and wealthier," he said. "If you're in the forty-fifth percentile and you fall to the fortieth percentile, there is no real palpable difference. If you're in the one-tenth of one percent and your kid falls to the top five percent, that's free fall. It's almost unimaginable." He added, "From the upper class, if you fall, there is a long way to go. Those good middle-class jobs have evaporated, so there aren't a lot of branches to hold on to on the way down." As Khan pointed out to me, it is easy to talk about opportunity for social and economic mobility in America, but it is harder for parents to accept that for someone else's child to rise from the bottom 25 percent to the top 10 percent, their child should have the same chance of falling that far. This fear of falling to a lower level is what motivates parents. I'm not sure if my wife and I ever thought about this fear so explicitly. But we want our daughters to have the best education possible, and what is saying something like that if not code for giving them opportunities to have as good a life as ours if not better, and to not fall below where they are starting?

Some people might be tempted to point out people who have dropped out of college and gone on to become fabulously successful and wealthy—from Bill Gates and Mark Zuckerberg to Justin Bieber's agent, Scooter Braun. But they all grew up in affluent homes with parents who were well educated and successful. They had been prepped to succeed. They also dropped out of top colleges. What's riskier is what Peter Thiel is doing with his stop-out-of-school initiative. Thiel, who has two degrees from Stanford and taught a class there in 2013, became a billionaire after founding PayPal and being the first outside investor in Facebook. His idea with stop out is to pay students to drop out of college—or never attend in the first place—and become entrepreneurs. It's a risky proposition. A few of the dropouts will make it big, but most, like entrepreneurial ventures themselves, will fail, burning through the $100,000, two-year fellowship with nothing to fall back on. All of the students could just as easily stay in college and test out their ideas like generations before them. On the other hand the students who apply are likely to be among the most driven in the world, with parents having funded their educational endeavors at a high level. One of Thiel's second group of fellows had been doing research at the Massachusetts Institute of Technology since he was thirteen, four years before he applied for a fellowship. Khan sees this kind of opportunity as one of the key advantages that children of affluent parents have over their peers. "In order to see an opportunity," he said, "you need to be positioned in a place where it's in your line of sight." In other words, Zuckerberg could more easily see Facebook from his Harvard dorm room than a rented triplex in Roxbury.

Does this mean low-income children, whose parents cannot afford this kind of education, are stuck at the bottom? Not necessarily. But they do have to be more careful and, to be honest, lucky. "If you're poor, single acts of unluck can wipe you out," Khan said. "You fail for a year in school and you're upper-middle-class, your parents hire a tutor and you're fine. You fail for a year as a poor kid and you get labeled an idiot, and chances are you start reacting negatively to education."

His worry is rooted in what it means to be an American, to embrace the myth of being self-made and to rise to wealth in a generation. That's what his father did. But Khan said he sees less of this today. He sees people, through great education, rise from being upper-middle-class to truly wealthy. That is far less inspiring than the mix-raced child born to a single mother becoming president of the United States. "If we lose this truly American thing—that is, you can become anything if you just work at it," he said, "then we're really going to lose what makes America America."

Beacham and Khan have two different views on spending money on education, but they are rooted in two popular veins of affluent thought on education—one content with public school bolstered by tutors; the other focused on the rewards and challenges of elite private schooling. But what if both are wrong and the secret to academic success comes much earlier? What if you started much younger and focused on skills that had nothing to do with tests and college? What if those girls at Westover who had been in a classroom since nursery school were the ones who had a better shot at being the CFO regardless of any extra classes like the one from Invest in Girls? And what if that approach to education was what made the difference in who was on the right side of the thin green line? If you ask James Heckman, a Nobel laureate, this is exactly how it works. And he has the data to back it up.

When Heckman was in school in the 1950s, he said his experience was nothing like what a smart, middle-class kid would go through today. He was left to his own devices by parents who were happy to let him explore what interested him. "I barely worked in high school," Heckman told me. "I grew up in Denver, so I could go outside a lot." His parents weren't negligent; few parents, he said, were paying attention back then. But Heckman considers himself lucky to have had parents who weren't overbearing and teachers who encouraged his interests. They didn't pressure him to do well on tests but instead allowed him to think. One teacher stood out, a landowner in southwest Colorado who came in to teach physics and inspired him to think differently. Frank Oppenheimer—brother of J. Robert Oppenheimer, who led the Manhattan Project, which created the atomic bomb—had lost his job at the University of Minnesota because he was a Communist and returned to his family's homestead in Colorado. "By a pure stroke of luck the principal of my school district asked him to teach just one class to students," said Heckman. "Oppenheimer had this deep love of experimental physics. He brought in this deep world of curiosity. To me I had never seen anything like it in my life."

The class wasn't just about physics, and certainly not about the type of physics needed to pass an advanced-placement exam. It was about experimentation in all of its forms. Heckman said he remembered listening to a Beethoven string quartet for the first time in Oppenheimer's class. "He had been rich and cultured, but he was just interested in everything," Heckman said. "He could discuss Nietzsche, culture, physics, and the latest space launch. Nothing was sacred and everything was discussed."

Heckman was smart, but more than that he was motivated. He read George Howe's *Mathematics for the Practical Man* and taught himself calculus at age thirteen. When he was living in Lexington, Kentucky, he took the new Iowa Skills Test and scored as if he were in the ninth month of twelfth grade. He was in seventh grade. "It was totally different," he said. "Nobody cared that much. But I was essentially a high school graduate. So they moved me ahead one year." Later, he was pretty sure his parents had no idea what he got on his SATs. ("They weren't stupid," he said. "They were high school graduates, but they were from a different generation.") It wouldn't have mattered if they did know. Heckman was bound for Colorado College on a scholarship for Coloradans. While Colorado College is a great school, it was not then, nor is it now, one of the country's elite colleges—probably not one that an eager tutor or private-school admissions officer would hold up as a model.

Yet Heckman has had a wildly successful life. Still fit in his late sixties when we met, he is one of the most influential economists of his generation, someone whose academic success translated into influence and wealth beyond academia. In 2000, he won the Nobel Prize in Economics for work that corrects for selection bias—when nonrandom information gets into a statistical study and skews it. An example often given is in trying to determine the link between education and wages: if you look only at people who have jobs and measure the link between years of education and earnings, you're missing a whole part of the population—those who are not working and who may have more or less education than those with jobs. The Heckman correction, as his discovery is known, provides a statistical way to consider information not part of that sample.

To noneconomists Heckman is better known for the work he has done on education, specifically on social interaction and what motivates children to succeed. He has looked at the issue not as an educator, sociologist, or psychologist but as an economist who wanted to determine which programs were most likely to create citizens who could contribute productively. His research has been varied. He has found that SAT scores are a fairly meaningless predictor of future success. Grades, he found, are better because they show students' ability to apply themselves over a longer period and to actually learn something. Another project showed why an employer might not want to hire someone with a GED. This finding surprised me. I would have thought that someone who dropped out of high school but then made the effort to get an equivalency degree would be motivated. Not so. "The essence of the GED is they're just as smart as high school graduates, but they're lacking in something basic," Heckman told me. "What we found is in a number of dimensions, the GEDs don't persist. They don't persist in marriage. They don't persist in the workplace. They don't persist in the Army. They don't persist in anything they do."

That presented a quandary: What to do with high school dropouts to improve their chances of success? Putting them in a classroom was a waste of time and money, he found. Training programs worked better because they forced the people to persist, to show up, to work, to get paid, and to come back the next day. That's far less glamorous than a program that turns a dropout into a poet, but the work-based programs have proved to be more effective. "If we try to boost the IQ of kids who are twenty years of age, it's going to be hard," he said. "Teaching kids or young adults social skills like staying on task, showing up on time, wearing a tie, and understanding the need to put together a CV—these lessons based on experience are highly valued."

All of this points to what Heckman called the malleability of behavior. It has a big implication for education. Changing soft skills can give a dropout a tremendous boost in the workplace, but it all depends on how the behavior is modified. "Alcoholics Anonymous and weight-loss clubs—they're horribly unsuccessful," Heckman said. "The change through those kinds of mechanisms doesn't work. But born-again Christians do work. Think of George Bush. There are plenty of people like him. It's teaching them a system of values and motivation."

What if you taught those social skills early on? What if you were able to work with malleable children the way job-training programs work with misguided adults? Would it affect their success and by extension their wealth? If you could get to these kids early on and in an effective way, Heckman found, it would improve a child's chance for meaningful success in life.

At the Perry Preschool in Ypsilanti, Michigan, in an experiment, the program took three- and four-year-old African-American children with IQs below 85 and worked on their social skills, giving them specific tasks to complete. At five, the children went to public school. When they were subsequently measured, the researchers found that their IQs had not improved but their social skills and their "outcomes" had. These students could stay more focused and do better with their cognitive skills when measured against a group of their peers who had not been in the program. The Perry project also succeeded in being rigorous about measuring apples to apples. It did not take a disadvantaged child and put him up against one whose family had far greater educational and financial resources. It measured him against similarly disadvantaged children and showed that working on social skills improved what he could do then and, as it turned out, later in life. According to Heckman and a coresearcher, Tim Kautz, these children had a lower propensity than peers who had not been in the program for "absences and truancies," "lying and cheating," "stealing," and "swears or use of obscene words." These may seem minor, but these traits help on achievement tests—which require studying to learn something—and in keeping at-risk children in school and in the workforce later.

"Success in life depends on personality traits that are not well captured by measures of cognition," Heckman and Kautz wrote about the Perry Preschool in "Hard Evidence on Soft Skills." "Conscientiousness, perseverance, sociability, and curiosity matter. While economists have largely ignored these traits, personality psychologists have studied them over the last century."

In the café at the Harris School of Public Policy, along the Midway in Chicago, Heckman asked me, "What did Perry do?" He paused. "That iconic program didn't raise IQs. What it did do was actually create soft skills. Kids were brought in a few hours a day for three years before they entered kindergarten. They were given a task every day. They were told, 'You have a project. You have to define the project. You have to execute the project. And then you have to review it collectively with your peers.' This wasn't a Baby Einstein project. They tried a strictly academic curriculum and it didn't work."

The study made me think about parents in upper-middle-class America who push their children to get into the top colleges when they themselves did not attend even a decent university. If they could apply the Perry criteria to their lives, they might look at the situation differently. They might assess the level of cognitive skills that they, the mother and father, passed on to their children and set expectations accordingly—not against a child whose parents are the top spinal surgeon in New York and a federal-court judge. What if, instead, the first set of parents worked more on the skills that lead to perseverance and determination, the traits that might allow their children to get ahead by outworking other students? What if they compared their children to how they themselves had done and hoped, as past generations did, to set them up to do a little bit better than they did—regardless of what their neighbors' kids did? Heckman's research would suggest that they would be able to raise kids who could find their way in the world—and not end up back on the family couch at twenty-five. These would be kids who could figure things out and not just regurgitate what they had been coached to memorize for a test.

As someone whose parents couldn't afford an SAT tutor but did well anyway, I always tried to outstudy everyone else in school and later outwork my peers. It would never have dawned on me not to persevere, to, in effect, quit. But in other ways I was as lucky as Khan suggested poor kids had to be: my mom had gone to a state teachers' college, my father had never even applied to college, my neighbors in Ludlow were thinking about surviving, not going to college, and I somehow didn't make any mistakes that derailed me. Not only was I left alone to study, but the bar was set incredibly low. Where I had a striking advantage was in two grandparents, Mamie and Papa, who took care of me after school. They supplied the type of focused attention early on, from healthy meals to constant talking, that Heckman found, in a study that tracked a hundred poor children in North Carolina for forty years, made a difference throughout life. Those babies from birth to age five randomly assigned to the group with better nutrition and stimulation performed better academically and in life and were also healthier and fitter as they aged. I had been randomly assigned to my mother's parents, and they made all the difference.

Since Heckman has two kids, I figured he was fair game to talk about how his own children have turned out. After all, Jean-Jacques

Rousseau, the eighteenth-century French philosopher, wrote eloquently about raising and educating children, but sent his own to orphanages. Heckman said his son and daughter went to the University of Chicago Laboratory Schools, an elite private school in Hyde Park, where the Obamas sent their girls when they lived there. Heckman was not enamored of it: "I felt it was somewhat unhealthy. It's high pressure, and that sort of pressure has to be stifling." This statement is remarkable from a professor at one of the most high-pressure universities in the world, one who might be expected to want his children to be put through a rigorous program. Quite the opposite. He regretted that the Lab School was so scheduled and regimented and that his children did not have the time he had had to sit and be alone. Still, his children have done quite well. They both graduated from top colleges, with his son earning a PhD in physics at Harvard and his daughter winning a Fulbright grant her senior year in college. "Both of my kids took to the academic life very well," Heckman said. "They were immersed in." But he did not come across as a parent who pushed his kids. If anything, he downplayed the role he had had in their academic success: "My wife and I tried to teach our kids a sense of values—not religious so much as ethical. Then we tried to relax. I didn't pay them for getting good grades. I didn't beat them over the head for not getting them. If they acted like rotten little kids, we told them." He added, "We set an example."

This does not happen in many affluent households where the focus is on the end: the great college. I asked Heckman, why did children seem to burn out in school so much more now? "It happens because it's a very structured existence," he said. "They haven't experimented. They haven't failed. Life is trial and error. But many of these kids are afraid to experiment. It gets to be very imbalanced, more so now with the emphasis on test scores. You need to learn that you can experiment and you can fail. Some of the most effective early-childhood programs have encouraged experimentation. They get kids to stay on task and solve novel problems."

Herein is the problem: too many parents will spend whatever amount of money it takes if the reward is a top private school and then the ideal college. With such a focus, they may be wasting their money and ruining their child's adolescence. Those parents who compete to send their three-year-olds to the best nursery schools are giving them the chance to learn how to stay on task and accomplish something—even if the parents are doing it for the wrong reasons. These early years are where children start learning the soft skills they will need to guide them through school and life. The parents may very well screw up their kids with their constant pressure to succeed at all costs. But they at least give their kids an educational foundation to lead a wealthy life. As the Jesuits said, "Give me the child until he is seven, and I will show you the man." That prescription may still be the best way to give your children the chance to live life on the wealthy side of the thin green line.

GIVE IT AWAY

THE ENTITLEMENT CONUNDRUM: WHAT REALLY RUINS KIDS

My wife and I spent a month and a half at our condo in Naples, Florida, in 2011 while we were renovating a couple of bathrooms in our house. It was right after my meeting with Tiger 21, and I could hear Tommy Gallagher, the banker with the barman's voice, telling me again and again that we didn't need our bright, simple condo. He was right, but Naples is a beautiful town on the Gulf of Mexico, where it's easy to be impractical. My wife's family has gone there since it was a beach town, long before it became a place where, as an old colleague put it, CEOs go to die. My wife's family has the real estate stories to prove it: her maternal grandmother bought her two-bedroom Michigan-style house with a one-room guesthouse on a canal for $45,000 in 1964; it was valued at $1.475 million when my wife's parents sold it in 2003 and well over $2 million when it was demolished in 2012 so a gigantic house that filled the entire lot could be erected. Losing that place full of memories was crushing to my wife. I pointed out one upside: the new house dwarfed the home of the jerk next door who used to tell my father-in-law that he needed to renovate his house. Naples can be like that, a type of perpetual one-upmanship on material success.

But it is also a town where retirees who generally have more money than they're going to spend before dying worry about their children's future and what they can provide them. Financially they're on the right side of the thin green line, but they have concerns for their children. Have they already given them too much? Should they invest in their newest idea? Were they fair to all of their children? How will their children fare without them? On that visit in 2011, we met a couple who lived across the canal from our condo and had a little boy whom our daughter found fascinating. We started hanging out and learned more about the couple. His father had the good fortune to open the town's first Mercedes-Benz dealership in the early 1980s and sell it at the end of the bull market in 2007. Our friend was rich by birth, and we realized that neither of the couple worked. It seemed they did nothing except sit at the beach, meet for drinks, and go to one of their clubs, where they were kind enough to pick up the tab—something that seems great but becomes odd after a few times. When we mentioned them to other friends, a story emerged. Our new friend had said his brother was living in central Florida, which I took to mean the horse country around Lakeland, given the family's wealth. Alas, he was in jail, sent away after a second beautiful girl died of a drug overdose in his bed. (The brother got a pass when the first beautiful girl was found dead next to him; accidents happen in wealthy beach towns.) I didn't like our new friend any less for this— what his brother did wasn't his fault—but he reminded me why both the adulation and the vilification of people who inherit vast sums of money miss the point. His brother had the financial resources people envy, and both brothers were financially secure for life. But their lives of leisure that can roll into bad decisions, if not death, were what many rich parents in Naples and similar places around the country worry about: Can too much money leave a child unmotivated? Our friend was also the type of kid that nonwealthy people hold up for derision—the trustafarian loafing away his days with fast cars, pretty women (turns out she was a girlfriend and the child was not his), and frosty-cold drinks. Yet I knew from my research that his problem had nothing to do with the money his parents had given him and everything to do with how they had presented their financial success to him when he was young.

How children perceive their parents' money and how they use it to define themselves is not demonstrably different whether it is $30,000 or $30 million. Someone with $30 million and a rampant sense of entitlement can afford the drugs and the louche lifestyle that leads to a couple of pretty girls dead in bed. Or in the good brother's case, a $1.8 million bungalow that he planned to tear down, a couple of $100,000 Mercedes-Benzes, and nothing to do all day. For the people with expectations around $30,000, the mistake could be having a child young with someone the person barely knows, maybe committing some petty crime, or just doing little in the expectation that the money could keep them going. When these issues come up, the children are called entitled or said to suffer from entitlement. They are seen as feeling entitled to things their parents worked for—usually financial but also connections—and that they inherited by the luck of their birth. In psychological circles, the term *sense of entitlement* is often used for a symptom of narcissistic personality disorder. It is defined as having "unreasonable expectations of especially favorable treatment or automatic compliance with his or her expectations." Randi Kreger, an expert on personality disorders, wrote in *Psychology Today* that someone suffering from this type of entitlement is "like a small child who never learned that she is not the center of the universe and throws tantrums when outsiders don't meet their narcissistic demands." Yet with some parent-child relationships, having a narcissistic sense of entitlement may be a natural reaction to being raised without boundaries and a sense of how the child's world compares to the wider one and the responsibilities the child has in it.

James Grubman, a psychologist and authority on how wealth impacts families, told me the ways to combat entitlement were not terribly difficult on the surface. First, parents needed to model gratitude and appreciation in their own lives; children needed to hear their parents say and show that they appreciated what they had. Second, the parents needed to walk their children through how the parents made a decision. Grubman gave the example of flying on a private plane. A younger child might wonder why the family didn't fly the same airlines as the child's friends; a teenage child might object to the jet as a waste of money and fuel. The parents needed to engage their children honestly, perhaps telling them that the parents chose to fly private as one way to spend their money, or that it was for security or a way to keep the family together. Explaining why you're flying private may seem like a problem most of us wish we had, but at its essence it is not any different from answering a child who asks why you're buying a new Toyota when your neighbor is still driving a much older one. The questions seem to be about money but they're really about values. Answering them incorrectly can have a damaging effect on children's understanding of where money comes from, how it is spent, and what they can expect to receive regardless of the parents' financial position. "Peter Buffett told me that watching his father enjoy his work was a very powerful model," Grubman said. "It was like he was saying, 'I've found what fits me and you need to persevere. I'm not going to tell you what your passion is, but it's a value in our family that no one is a slacker.'"

Even when parents think they have planned for everything that could pull children apart, more often than not they have just planned for the financial part—usually, transferring assets and paying the tax bill. A few summers before we renovated our house, we took a vacation to a resort in Chatham, Massachusetts, a pretty town on Cape Cod. One morning we drove into town to get breakfast. Our daughter wasn't yet a year old, and at the restaurant an older woman, whose kids were grown and gone, struck up a conversation with my wife. The woman was nostalgic for when her kids were our daughter's age. She gave us advice on what not to miss. Probably because I was reading the Saturday *New York Times,* where my column runs, my wife told her what I did, and the woman said she had read my column that morning. She remembered another column that people often recall, about a battle between two wealthy people over the location of a stone wall in Westport, Connecticut—one of my finer forays into how money can fuel a silly dispute. This memory triggered her to tell me about her plan for her beach house, which had been in her family for two generations. She was going to leave it equally to her two sons so they would always come back to it. Didn't I think that was a great idea? Normally I dodged these conversations, but maybe because of the sea air or a spike in my blood sugar from the sweet glaze on my scone, I told her that I thought it was an awful idea. She was taken aback.

I tried to explain. What did her kids do? One was a teacher, the other had a Wall Street job. Were they married? The teacher was married to a teacher and had a kid or two. The other had just married his third wife. Did the boys get along? Of course they did. What about their spouses? Well . . . Who was going to pay for the upkeep? They'd split it, the woman piped up, showing me she had thought about this possibility. For how long would that be possible for the teacher? What would he do when his brother wanted to put a new cedar-shake roof on the house or redo the kitchen with high-end appliances and cabinetry? Would he ask his brother for the equivalent of a year's salary for his half of the renovation cost? She couldn't answer these questions, but she wasn't alone. Most people don't think such things out: they focus on the beauty of the home and their memories of it. Maybe she could leave some money for the house's upkeep? Well, she didn't have that kind of money. The house was her biggest asset. Then, I said, she should sell it and split the money between them. This outcome was unacceptable to her. She didn't want the house to leave her family, and she couldn't fathom that giving them money and letting the Wall Street brother invite the teacher brother to his own beach house would be better for family harmony when she was gone. Could the brothers make it work? Anything's possible, but the odds were against them. It would go fine for a while. Then it wouldn't. The shift would be slow. Both brothers would want to use the house on the Fourth of July with their family, but only one could fit. The brother who was footing all the bills for the upkeep would feel entitled to more of it over time. The brother who could never maintain the house on his own would think that this scenario was not what their mother would have wanted. Then, when the spouses weighed in about who was paying for the house or what the mother's wishes had been, it would get challenging.

Ask any financial adviser and he will tell you this happens all the time. Was it the value of the house that did this to them? The beach location? Absolutely not. It was who was entitled to use it and when. But to most people looking at it, the cause of the strife would be money. It's not true. If the house had been sold and the money divided between the brothers, it would not split them apart: each would have his half to do with as he wanted. Their mother's hope was that the house, in a way cash could never do, would keep them together. This woman's thinking is understandable, but flawed. Parents want to provide for their children equally. Children who grew up spending summers in Chatham, with its mix of wealth, affluence, and free-spending tourists, would have been exposed to many of the world's opportunities. It shouldn't have come as a surprise to the son who became a teacher that working in education offers many rewards but a high salary is not one of them, any more than it should not have been a surprise to the other brother that the long hours, travel, and adrenaline rush of finance are not always conducive to stable marriages. "Parents make the mistake of wanting to be the provider of money," Grubman said. "It goes all the way back to childhood and allowances. If a child wants to go off to Guatemala or wherever, they need to have some skin in the game. The mistake many wealthy families make is to subsidize it." The beach house was no different: the mother was trying to subsidize her one son's participation in the house at the expense of the other. It wouldn't end in the way she hoped.

So what can people do to prevent an inheritance—or the expectation of one—from leading to problems with a child or among siblings? First, parents have to understand that their indulgences can create three types of inheritors: flaneurs, sheltereds, or inspireds. At first glance it may seem that only the last group of inheritors is acceptable—we all want our children to go forth inspired about what they're doing—but it's not so simple. Being any of these three can push a child onto the wrong side of the thin green line. Of course, the parents, for all of their money, may have never been on the right side of that line to start with, so it's hard to expect more from their children.

Sitting at a sleek restaurant in New Orleans, waiting for the lunch menus to arrive, Randy Fertel offered within minutes of meeting me that he was pretty sure money had ruined his family. "I've watched it do a lot of harm," he said. His mother, Ruth Fertel, founder of Ruth's Chris Steak House, built a company worth hundreds of millions of dollars and kept it based in New Orleans. That kind of money has enabled Fertel and his older brother to do whatever they want in life; it also gave them semiroyalty status in the city itself, though they remained little known beyond it. Fertel, a full-figured bon vivant and retired literature professor, feels he did the most with the advantages he was given, though as he sees it, his life wasn't easy.

Fertel is a flaneur. He is representative of a group of inheritors who live nice, comfortable lives that seem enviable from the outside but come with their own challenges. The top one is that most everyone else they know has less freedom and more financial concerns and cannot imagine how life couldn't be great for them. Fertel was given tens of millions of dollars for doing nothing more than being born to the founder of a national chain of steak houses. In addition to teaching college literature classes—mostly, it seems, as a low-paid adjunct professor—he used his inheritance to indulge his passions. When I remarked on his watch, he said it was a Patek Philippe, a beautiful watch that costs $20,000 or more. I asked if someone had given it to him or if it marked a milestone. "No," he said, "there's just a great watch store here. I also collect pens." Money should have liberated Fertel, but he associated it with the problems his family has had, particularly his bumpy childhood. For many flaneurs, so many opportunities mean they struggle to focus on any of them. Those who can, as Fertel did with literature, still lack the spark that propels the most successful people, such as his mother. If you have such a large cushion, what is going to drive you? If not money, maybe recognition, but if that never comes to fruition, a flaneur's fallback plan is still better than most people's life goal.

Fertel's story, while as unique as anything else that happens in New Orleans, is a cautionary tale for any parent, wealthy, rich, or neither. Fertel was the younger of two sons born to Rodney and Ruth Fertel. At the beginning, the father had all the money, from his own father, who had parlayed his success with a pawnshop on Rampart Street into real estate and other investments. He left a portion of that money to Fertel's father at twenty-one, and Rodney realized he did not have to work and didn't. "He wanted to be a coach," said Fertel, whose girth and wavy hair make him look every bit a New Orleans hedonist. "He never did anything. He didn't become a coach, which he would have been good at. Instead he became a life coach for people who didn't want one. He had all of these wild ideas." Of all of Rodney's wild ideas, the most famous was the promise he made when running for mayor of New Orleans in 1969: if elected, he would get a gorilla for the zoo. He lost the race, but he donated two gorillas, Molly and Scotty, to the zoo. Fertel's mother, Ruth, was pragmatic by comparison. She saw an ad for a steak house by a horse track and bought it for $18,000 in 1965. She got the money by borrowing $22,000 against her home, which had come to her in the course of a ten-year divorce from Fertel's father. At her banker's suggestion she borrowed extra money to have working capital to pay for the inventory. ("She always gave him credit for her success," Fertel said. "She had an easier time giving credit to those at some distance than those near to her.") Ruth proved savvy. She had asked the previous owner, a guy named Chris, to stay on for a month to teach her about the business, but she realized he was trying to sabotage her by buying cheap meat, overcooking it, and seasoning it differently. She fired him. Ruth took that one restaurant and turned it into four others in New Orleans, giving them all the same unwieldy name, Ruth's Chris Steak House. Ten years after she got into the business, she began franchising. By the time she died in 2002 at age seventy-five, the chain had grown to eighty-two steakhouses. She had been out of the business since she sold it to a private-equity company in 1999, a move that made her and her sons fantastically rich.

If you take out the wealth, Fertel's life has had normal ups and downs. He wasn't the best student in high school—he welcomed the chance to work in his mother's restaurants and avoid doing homework—but he ended up at American University in Washington, DC, and then Harvard, where he earned a PhD in English literature. He spent time between college and graduate school living and studying in Paris. In 1975, he married and a few years later began to have children. He worked as a professor at various small colleges—jobs that paid modestly. The pay didn't matter since his mother subsidized him. His relationship with his father was rocky and intermittent, but not so different from mine or that of many other men. Again, though, most people would have to look hard to see the pain amid the pleasure. One of Fertel's great fights with his father happened when Fertel was studying in Paris and his father invited him to come down to Majorca for a vacation with his brother, just back from Vietnam. "How do you turn down Majorca?" Fertel told me. "I went down there and immediately starting fighting with Dad."

Fertel had a flawed sense of money. In a striking passage in his memoir about his parents, *The Gorilla Man and the Empress of Steak,* he wrote about flying to Zurich at age thirty-four to meet his father in 1984. "My salary at Le Moyne College in Syracuse had grown from $15,000 to $21,000 in three years of teaching. With two kids and expensive tastes, we weren't managing." His trip to see his father was not to reconcile, but to get a bailout. "I felt hemmed in, desperate to keep the profession I loved but couldn't afford if I stayed in the marriage. Although I hadn't seen my father in six years, I found myself in Zurich, desperate for a small stipend that would enable me to maintain my life. Dad had the wherewithal. Would he have the generosity?" His father wouldn't give him any money, but he did pay for an injection of fetal lamb cells, which were meant to make you more youthful. Fertel ended up returning to New Orleans to work for his mother, which lasted until 1989, when she had another employee fire him. A year later, his wife divorced him as he was recovering from surgery to remove a brain tumor. His mother had also stopped talking to him.

It wasn't a great first forty years, but he had something most men with bad childhoods, work histories, marriages, and health problems do not: money. After his mother made a series of bad real estate investments, Ruth's Chris Steak House was put into a trust, which was 80 percent owned by Fertel and his brother. That meant he could continue teaching as an adjunct professor in New Orleans and New York without ever worrying about money to support himself. When the company was sold, he said of his mother, "She made me rich, kind of by accident." And rich he was.

The one upside he saw in his rocky relationship with his parents was it drove him to get away from them—though they were always supporting him. "My passion for literature came from growing up in this totally dysfunctional family," he said. "I wasn't getting any parenting so I went to books for parenting and maybe for wisdom. And somehow, out of that came this great passion for literature and writing and teaching." He withdrew and his interest in literature became the center of his universe. But his parents' money was what allowed him to continue to pursue his love of literature without worrying about making a living. In talking to him, I didn't get any sense that his parents would have been any better at being actual parents had they been broke. They seemed too selfish for that. Money doesn't make people good or bad parents. Engagement in a child's life determines that. Money just buys things a child needs or wants. And money doesn't turn children into flaneurs: distracted parents who use money to make up for their lack of involvement do. In a parental void, money can at least buy the trappings of family life, such as heirloom watches bought with his own money.

What happens to children takes time. Randi Kreger noted one of the symptoms of a sense of entitlement is the feeling that "my needs have priority, and if others don't like it they just don't understand my superiority." On some level, Fertel realized that had he been a poor kid from New Orleans, he would not have studied in Paris or gone to Harvard for his PhD. Yet in his day-to-day life, he clearly believed that money had caused him problems, when in reality it had given him a more comfortable financial life than he would otherwise have had. The money was a source of support where his parents were not, though he does not see it that way. He was not unlike so many children of financiers or successful businesspeople who hold forth on the evils of money—the same money that paid for them to grow up in a nice neighborhood and attend fine schools. What they are really complaining about is the absence of their parents, who were working long hours to make the money they felt they needed.

As we wrapped up our lunch, Fertel pushed a piece of paper across the table, saying, "Let me give you this." It was a letter he had written to his two sons when he set up their trust, which contained $7 million. Throughout lunch, Fertel had been both wary and forthcoming about his sons. I told him I wouldn't quote from the letter, but I didn't have to worry about that. Fertel told me everything that was in it.

"The trust had been a source of a lot of conflict and pain in my life," he told me. "So it was troubling to create one for them, but it was the right thing to do. So I wrote a piece about that. There are finance people who have read it and said, 'Randy, this is the best statement I've ever seen on the problem of wealth,' so I was really proud of that."

His sons, he said, did not see the letter that way. "When I gave it to them, their response was 'This is so controlling.' It was the *worst* possible response. I thought it was really going to be helpful."

Fertel was baffled that his children did not see the trust in the same way he did—as a great start in life, as something that could let them do whatever they wanted. "We tried to explain this is not going to be enough money for you," he said, betraying no hint of irony that he was talking about $7 million. "You're going to need a job. This is not going to carry you. But they heard exactly the opposite." I'll admit to being baffled that he didn't think $7 million was enough money for his kids to live on, given that it had fifty years to grow. Unless Fertel's sons had no money skills whatsoever, a trust with $7 million that grew at 5 percent a year would allow them to take out $371,753 per year until they were eighty and not run out of money. Or, if they were more aware of inflation, they could take out $175,000 a year and maintain the same buying power for fifty years with an annual 2.5 percent increase for inflation—when fifty years hence they would take out $618,000. Not being able to live within that amount was, of course, the problem. And from the conversation it seemed that he was setting his boys up to be another generation of flaneurs, whatever their aspirations might be.

When I later read the letter, I found it more overwritten than compelling. Fertel had studied great writers and he loved literature. But trying to fill a letter about trusts with literary allusions confused his message. That his children found it controlling was more a function of what they read into the letter than what it said: he felt that people who had a passion in life were happier, and he wanted them to use their twenties to find that passion and prepare for receiving the money. Mostly, though, the letter read as if Fertel had written it to his younger self. He tried to use his experiences to keep his sons from the pain he had felt from his father and mother, who used money as a means of reward and control. A trust, he felt, would allow his sons to skip over the tough part of life—acquiring money to fund their passion—and go right to the more enjoyable and, he hoped, meaningful part: pursuing that passion. Both sons have aspirations to write for television and film.

"I kind of despair," he told me. "They're both trying to write their way into Hollywood. They're both very smart and very talented. Maybe it will happen."

He added, "They've both had entitlement issues. That's the main thing to overcome, to prevent."

I had enjoyed Fertel's company and I appreciated his candor and thoughtfulness. But I left the restaurant thinking that his boys were just modeling themselves after him. One of the tests James Grubman does with parents struggling with entitlement issues is to ask them if they have taught their children how to tip. Naturally, he said, they all balk. Of course they have. But then he asks them to show how they tip someone. "There's a difference between 'Here's your tip' and 'Thank you very much, sir,'" he said. "Kids know the difference in the behaviors of tipping. It's about showing respect." I don't know how Fertel tipped. I paid for lunch since he didn't reach for the bill.

Walking around New Orleans after lunch, I thought of a conversation I had had in early 2000 with the novelist Kurt Vonnegut. I had spotted him, a bushy-haired curmudgeon, on the Amtrak platform in Springfield, Massachusetts. As the train made its way to New York, I walked back to find him, hoping to have the courage to talk to him. To my surprise, he slid over. We started chatting. He said he had spent some time in nearby Northampton recovering from a fire that had engulfed his town house in New York. Seventy-seven at the time, he was worried about people becoming uninteresting.

"The whole excitement of life is becoming," he told me. "Becoming is the process by which a person becomes a person, or an artist an artist."

To start miles ahead of everyone else may sound wonderful, but without any understanding of the work it took to get there does a disservice to children, young and old. Money that is just doled out can rob people of the excitement of "becoming." Parents who make sure they don't rob their children of that opportunity to become whatever they are going to be is one divider of people who are wealthy and rich. When it comes to inheritance, it is far more pervasive than that. Channeling your good fortune to help your children get a good education is laudable, but using it to make sure they do not fail is a path to future failure.

Naomi Sobel was a different case. She had every educational advantage and opportunity a parent could want for a child. She went to the exclusive Spence School in Manhattan and on to the University of Chicago, and Columbia University for graduate school. Now a petite young woman with big brown eyes and an easy smile, she lives in Somerville, Massachusetts, near Boston. She works at a nonprofit to which she had originally donated money, having started off in publishing. What she does financially matters little. "Any paid work I do is by choice," she told me. "I have enough money that I don't ever have to work." After living in New York after school, she moved to the Boston area because a girl she was dating was going to the Massachusetts Institute of Technology. She never thinks about money in terms of what she needs to live. She thinks about it in terms of how her money can effect change. Yet not until her freshman year in college did she realize she was wealthy. In this, she is a sheltered inheritor—well educated, smart, but out of touch with the world the rest of us live in. It's not uncommon. In an effort to keep children motivated, parents shelter children from their wealth, as best they can. But what often happens is that the children find out about the money in a crisis and have no idea what to do with it. It is not unlike parents of middle-class children who don't talk about money and leave their kids to guess about how much they have when they might have far less. While financially someone like Sobel is always going to be on the right side of the thin green line, emotionally she and other sheltereds struggle with wealth they don't understand.

"It turns out the only person who didn't know I had money was me," she told me. "There are a lot of things that growing up I didn't see as class signifiers." Such as her mother's town house with an elevator in it.

Sobel's family wealth comes from a natural-resources company that her grandfather sold to General Electric. She categorized her mother as comfortable until the company sold. Then her wealth skyrocketed. Sobel's father came from a middle-class family and worked first in advertising and then as a teacher. It fell to him to talk to her about money and values as a girl. "He tried to teach me how to fit into the world," she said. "My mom didn't feel comfortable talking about money." He took her to the New York public school where he taught and sent her away to summer camp with people from all different social classes. When she went off to college, her parents sat her down and asked her how much she thought she needed for spending money. They wanted her to have a budget, something they had never talked about. So she came up with a number, admitting she had no idea if it was too much or enough. Then her grandfather died and her mother flew out to see her. Her parents had by then divorced, so her mother sat her down. "Here was this big number and I didn't know where it put me," she told me. "I didn't know if it was enough to buy a house. It turns out it was enough to buy many very nice houses." A credit to her parents, though, she kept at what she was doing in college—studying, dating, working at her summer job.

Her confusion around money accelerated after she graduated. She had done well and was applying for various jobs when it dawned on her that she had no idea what to ask for a salary—nor even what people earned. This seems impossible to believe for almost anyone who isn't a sheltered, but think about all the things we take for granted as we get older and our world gets smaller: Can everyone know the price of a postage stamp? Money allows you not to know. "No one ever talked about it [money]," she said. "I didn't know what my dad made as a teacher or my mom from investments. I didn't know what my friends made, and I was embarrassed to ask them. I didn't know if I could draw on my assets. I didn't know if I should. I didn't know what my costs were. I didn't have a budget. I was embarrassed." One thing that stuck with her was somebody telling her that your housing costs should be about a quarter to a third of your income. When she did the math, she freaked out and moved back home with her mother. She can joke about this now and also about her first job: "I ended up doing fund-raising, which was ironic because I didn't understand money and I was afraid of it." But through this experience she started to see her good fortune. Money could effect social change, and she had lots of it.

When the Occupy Wall Street protests started, she joined them by announcing she was the One Percent. She sided with the protesters on the need to increase taxes on herself and her family. She said she was particularly bothered that her salary was taxed at a higher rate than her investments, for which she did no work. But it wasn't an easy decision for her. She worried in a way that most rebellious twentysomethings would not. "I e-mailed everyone in my family that I was going to do it," she told me. "It helps that we don't share last names. My mom and I are the only Sobels who have a lot of money." In this, the weight of her wealth, all that she was entitled to receive from her grandfather's work, clouded her decision-making. In her shelteredness, she asked permission to rebel. It wasn't limited to her family. Her friends, knowing or suspecting her background, questioned what she was doing. "I had some great conversations with friends, some of whom were challenging me about it," she said. "They weren't challenging me about my wealth. They were challenging me about policy issues." Yet, the very material privilege that she was questioning brought her sacred advantages. The Boston protests in 2011 fell during Yom Kippur, one of the high Jewish holidays. She got a Torah scroll lent to her so the group could celebrate in Dewey Square. Torahs are fantastically expensive since every one is handwritten from another Torah that has been deemed kosher; any mistake means the transcriber has to start over from the beginning.

Sobel has become more comfortable helping friends in need and talking about class privilege. "It's one of the marks of privilege that you don't have to know how much things cost," she said. "When I got my first cell phone, price didn't come into it—the discussion was about responsibility and my curfew." Still, she seemed bothered that she wasn't on the right path yet. But how many other twenty-eight-year-olds have everything figured out? If not for the tens of millions of dollars in her bank account, there would be little pressure on her to have any answers. An apartment of her own in a town like Somerville, a girlfriend, and a job she liked would be fine. That she has had several jobs since graduate school wouldn't matter. My first eighteen months out of graduate school I had three jobs, but my friends just made fun of me. I was figuring it out. The difference was I had no backstop, save the occasional hundred bucks my grandfather sent me. Taking time off to think through what I wanted to do wasn't an option. But for young inheritors like Sobel, the expectation is that they should have life figured out at an earlier age by dint of their wealth and privilege. This expectation is tough. Money does not make people mature about financial matters—having less money is more likely to do that since children will hear parents discussing financial issues more often and deeply in the home—nor does it grant people answers that are only learned, if we're lucky, through years of experience.

Sobel is plagued by another burden: the need to do something meaningful in life with all the money she has inherited. "I feel extremely fortunate that some of the inheritance I've received has come during my parents' life and they're here to talk about it," she told me. "It's a question of legacy and loyalty and not wanting to mess it up." (Speaking of it, she can make inheriting a huge amount of money seem like no fun at all.) Given her intelligence and drive, she was not likely to turn out like my flaneur neighbor in Naples. But as a sheltered, she faced risks: naïveté about money, feelings about wealth that could be stultifying if not paralyzing, concerns about self-worth. Like many wealthy people I have spoken to over the years, she seemed trapped by the responsible rich person's psalm of obligation: "To those to whom much is given, much is expected."

Eight years into knowing of her wealth, Sobel said she attributed her comfort around her inheritance to a support group for young inheritors called Resource Generation. (Yes, there are support groups for people who are young, rich, and struggling with how to combine the two.) The group helped her come to terms with her money, which was something she felt she could not talk about with anyone who wasn't wealthy. How could they understand? She reminded me of Les Quick, the son of the founder of Quick & Reilly, who talked about why he joined an investment club such as Tiger 21 when he couldn't run out of money: "I needed me time, eleven times a year, and that was really it." For Sobel, it was similar: she can joke as an adult that she didn't think it was odd to grow up in a Greenwich Village town house with its own elevator since her friends lived in vast Park Avenue apartments.

Yet she was struggling with what the psychologist Barry Schwartz calls the paradox of choice. Having unlimited options should be a great thing. Instead of choosing between two things or even among three or four, you have a hundred options—and all of them are good. "If we're rational," Schwartz wrote in his book *The Paradox of Choice*, "added options can only make us better off as a society. Those of us who care will benefit, and those of us who don't care can always ignore the added options. This view seems logically compelling; but empirically, it isn't true." He cited a famous study on selecting jars of jam in a gourmet grocery store. When people were shown twenty-four jars of jam, they purchased one 3 percent of the time; when they were shown only six, they bought a jar 30 percent of the time. In both cases, the number of jams available to taste was the same, but the appearance of greater choice overwhelmed people into doing nothing. "Filtering out extraneous information is one of the basic functions of consciousness," Schwartz wrote. "If everything available to our senses demanded our attention at all times, we wouldn't be able to get through the day." The same could be said for a sheltered inheritor who had the wealth and education to do absolutely anything in the world. She could evaluate every single option and end up doing nothing. Or she could choose one but second-guess herself and wonder, given her wealth and pedigree, if she hadn't squandered her privilege. Even if she is successful by most measures, she probably won't be as successful as critics think she should be with the advantages she has. In this, Sobel's choice to take herself out of the economic race and devote herself to nonprofit work may be the most rewarding and potentially satisfying option for her, even though every option was open.

It is easy to dismiss the problems of people who inherent money. Sobel could become a do-gooder because she'd never have to worry about paying her rent, let alone funding a retirement plan. And if Fertel and his sons blow through the money his mother made, who cares? They are a democracy's version of royalty: anointed with riches simply by the accident of their birth. The last thing the rest of us want to hear is any griping about what curmudgeons mom and dad were or how overwhelmingly large the number on the brokerage statement is. But that type of thinking makes money something it is not and should never be: something more than a means of exchange. It conflates money that is inherited with less tangible attributes such as happiness and fulfillment. What people with a lot of money, whether earned, inherited, or filched, have is more financial freedom than people with less money. But financial freedom, even the kind that puts you securely on the safe side of the thin green line, is not the same as happiness or contentment or generosity or freedom itself. Most people can imagine how much better their life would be with some sum of money, how it would free them and allow them to travel and be all-around happier people. What such thinking misses is that money without some purpose in life is soul-sapping. Ruth Fertel became so rich because she loved the restaurant business. As her son told me, she was a gambler, and money was her way of keeping score. She checked the totals on every check and did the math in her head for bills reaching thousands of dollars. She knew viscerally where and how she was making money. Most heirs who struggle in life lack that connection to how the inheritance came to them: they just see what it bought their parents and imagine what it can buy them. At worst, they become entitled; at best, they feel guilty that by the luck of their birth, they have no worries about the thing that keeps most of us going: earning enough money to afford what we need and want.

When I think of problems with inheritance I don't limit it to the rich or the wealthy, nor do I associate it with money alone. The problem is the sense of entitlement that puts you at the center of the world—either as a Falstaffian bon vivant or a brilliant but conscience-wracked do-gooder. It can rob you of motivation whatever the sum involved. So why when it comes to inheritance is there still so much anxiety on one side and envy on the other? Most of us don't begrudge professional athletes their enormous paychecks unless they fail to perform on the field. We've become inured to gigantic contracts. But we're quick to judge sports stars who have little education around money if they lose it all. There's a disconnect. They're entitled in that they have always been great athletes and coddled because of their ability. Money gave them the feeling that they could relax and spend because it would always be there like the adulation they felt growing up. Then it's gone and they are no longer the center of their universe, something that is difficult to accept after many decades. That is the essence of entitlement. It is the difference between being grateful for what you have and feeling the world has ensured that you will always have it no matter what.

Roy O. Williams, a portly former San Francisco 49ers football player whose son and grandson played in the National Football League, is the dean of dealing with delinquent families. Now slightly thicker around the middle but no less imposing in his seventies, Williams has distilled the parental worries about inheritance and entitlement to its essence. "How do I give my children the benefit of my money and not have it impact them in a negative way?" he told me. His business is helping parents answer that question. In our conversation, he alluded to what I think is the more pressing problem: how these adults were indulged as children. He makes parents ask themselves what is the long-term purpose of their wealth and corrects anyone who starts talking like an accountant. "If you don't define it as money and things but as our values and the confidence we have in our children, that's a huge, huge opportunity," Williams said in his soft mumble. "It's not the money. It's never the money. It's family love and togetherness. Imagine if you could have family love and togetherness for generations?" That would constitute freedom for many people: the money would be there, but so, too, would all the support that is lacking in people who have a sense of entitlement or feel adrift because of their privilege.

Research shows that holding on to money will be hard for anyone who didn't make it. Jay Zagorsky, of the Center for Human Resource Research at Ohio State University, has found in an analysis of data that tracked people in their twenties, thirties, and forties that the money disappeared for 35 percent of those who received an inheritance. Whatever they spent it on, it did not increase their wealth. For someone to save at least some of their inheritance, the amount had to be at least $100,000, he told me. "My research shows the typical person spends half of their inheritance," he said. That the money disappears is not a surprise to anyone who has looked at people who inherit it. In his book *Preparing Heirs: Five Steps to a Successful Transition of Family Wealth and Values*, Roy Williams listed phrases in various languages about how quickly money is lost between generations—all a version of shirtsleeves to shirtsleeves in three generations.

While worrying about what money will do to children sounds like a high-class problem, it isn't. What constitutes wealth—especially to give someone a sense of security but not entitlement—is relative. Franco Lombardo, another family consultant, said his goal is to distill a family's issues onto a single piece of paper, taking a strategy from Toyota's management book. On one side he writes out the current reality, on the other the desired reality. His job is to get the two squared up. But his years in this business have taught him that a family's problems around money can generally be summed up in a top-ten list: guilt around having money; fear of responsibility; sense of entitlement; feeling above the law or society in general; feeling burdened or shamed by the money; being disconnected from reality; feeling isolated and lonely; misusing money to control and manipulate other people; undermining the personal drive of the person you're trying to help with your money; and harboring a deep fear of being taken advantage of by others. It's a laundry list of financial horrors. But the individual feelings have less to do with actual dollar amounts and more to do with perceptions of wealth. Avoiding the traps of entitlement is both harder and more obvious than most people imagine.

The inspired inheritors are a class of kids who are driven in spite of their family's wealth. They don't need to work as hard as they might, but they do nonetheless. Doug Ideker is the father of two inspireds. Long before he had any money, he knew that he had to model behavior for his boys. Ideker, a bald, barrel-chested man, started a building-supply company with his brother-in-law and ran it for eighteen years, expanding to four locations around Colorado. "We both had sons, but I had always encouraged my sons not to go into the family business and find their own career path," he told me. More than not encouraging them, Ideker gave them an ultimatum as soon as they were old enough to get summer jobs: either find one on their own or go to work at the loading dock at 6:30 a.m., where they would report to a supervisor. "They didn't like the six thirty a.m. idea, but I can tell you they both worked for me at various times in their high school and college years. They said it was a good experience. I made everyone know that they didn't work for me. They had a supervisor and I never intervened. They had to be accountable for what they did when they were on the clock." Ideker did this as much to build his sons' character as to maintain morale at his company: he knew that if he gave his sons advantages over other employees, it would hurt his sons in the long run, but it would also hurt his business if his longtime employees felt resentment.

After working long hours and earning a high salary for decades, Ideker and his brother-in-law sold their company in 2003. "We never intended on selling out—we intended on running it ourselves," Ideker said. It was an offer they couldn't refuse and it was also good timing since his clients were building contractors and who knows what would have happened to the business in the 2007 housing collapse. After the sale, Ideker had enough money never to work again. He was wealthy. But not yet fifty, he was worried about that. "Before the sale, sure, they saw that we had a successful business, but they also saw how many hours I worked, they saw the sacrifices that I made taking time away from the family," he told me. "All of a sudden that stopped and there was this pool of money sitting there and they saw me throttle back. It would have been easy for them to think, 'Hey, this is pretty good.' To their credit, they never thought that way."

To compound his worries, his sons were twenty and twenty-four at the time, one still in college, the other not yet on his own. Instead of hiding anything, Ideker and his wife, Terrie, went for radical transparency. They told them everything they had. They also told them the vast amount that was going to charity. What was left for the sons could be used to pay for college and graduate school, but not for them to become "professional students," as Ideker put it. He wanted them to have goals in life whatever they might be, but he wanted those goals to have an economic benefit. "They needed to be responsible citizens," he told me. For guidance, Ideker sought out an adviser called SEI Private Wealth to lend some collective intelligence to his endeavor. "People often talk about the values around money," said Jeff Ladouceur, one of his advisers. "They want their kids to think about other people and they want them to be entrepreneurs. That's a lot of talk. The more I talk, the more my kids zone me out. If I exemplify the action, they seem to get it quicker." Ideker worked hard, but so do teachers, gardeners, and factory workers without becoming rich. He was passionate about doing something that was also worth a lot to someone else.

While a financial firm was necessary to work out the technical aspects of wealth—trusts, tax planning, charitable giving—Ideker's success lay in things far from this arcane world. He had raised two boys who were inspired to do their own thing, even though their parents would probably leave them enough money to coast. How did he do this? One, Ideker led by example. Two, he was religious, so he had a set of values that he could transmit to his children. Three, he and his wife gave back to their community. They showed their kids what it meant to be wealthy even before they had so much money that they didn't have to work. He worried about his kids being productive and self-sufficient, but he and his wife had modeled the behavior—reinforced by their values—that had propelled their boys into careers that would allow them to make their own money and establish their sense of self-worth. While the kids had a cushion, they were taught the crucial connection between labor and lifestyle.

When we spoke, both of his sons were working in real estate. They were also involved in charities of their choosing. The older one was focused on one that funded housing for teenage mothers and basketball camps for at-risk children. The younger one was setting up his own charity that would pay off student loans for people who wanted to work in the ministry or other nonprofits. Ideker said he struggled with how he and his wife had parented before and after their windfall, but he kept coming back to one phrase: *enable, don't command.* "We've never tried to force anything on them," he told me. "Everything we've tried to do has involved enabling them in a very positive way." He added, "The other part is review, review, review. When there is a new event in our life or our sons' lives, we sit down and talk about it and ask what happened, why it happened, what the impact was. We do that as a family and we don't glaze over that." Such open and honest communication, Lombardo found in his research, was the key to success. It also put inheriting kids on the right side of the thin green line because they came to see the good things money could provide while still appreciating how hard it was to earn and save.

8

HOW DID GIVING MONEY AWAY BECOME DIFFICULT?

On an overcast but otherwise perfect late-spring day, I approached the Stanwich Club—one of the best golf courses in America and the finest country club in Greenwich, Connecticut—with a bit of trepidation. There are private clubs and then there are *private* clubs, and it was the latter. The barely marked entrance to Stanwich still bares the name of the estate it once was. I drove carefully down the long, narrow driveway to the well-shaded clubhouse. When I was flagged to stop, a cluster of caddies, all black men, took my clubs out of my car and checked my name off a list. They handed me a bright-green shirt with the course's logo—a witch flying on a golf flag—a pin to show my support for the troops, and instructions on where lunch was being served and where I could hit balls to loosen up before the tournament. As I walked to the patio, I was amazed at how beautiful the grounds and buildings were. If you think golf is an exclusionary sport for rich people, Stanwich is the type of club that confirms your belief. But if you love the game of golf, Stanwich is the type of course where you would immediately start wondering how to finagle another invite. I was in the latter camp.

I was there to play in the second annual Jonas Center for Nursing Excellence Golf Tournament, a charity event that had attracted about seventy golfers that year. The group was a mix of injured veterans, nurses supported by Jonas Center grants, and a circle of hedge-fund analysts and executives. There was a retired general who had been in charge of all nurses in the Army and a famous golf professional who had a show on the Golf Channel. At the center of it all were three people: Donald and Barbara Jonas, who would celebrate their sixtieth wedding anniversary the next day, and George Fox, the member who made the venue possible. Fox was a bronzed, fit, and handsome Southerner. He had made his fortune running a fund of hedge funds, a company that pooled clients' money so it could be parceled out into hedge funds that his clients, rich as they were, would not be able to get into on their own. Fox was as slick as the Jonases were staid. Mr. Jonas was tall, bald, and had the slight belly of a man in his eighties; his handshake was quick and firm. He looked like a kind grandfather, though he retained the sharpness of a man who was self-made. His fortune came from a chain of kitchenware stores called Lechters. His wife, in her wide, oval sunglasses and blown-out, blond hair, was glamorous in the way of old Hollywood stars. It was the spring of 2013 and they greeted me like a friend. It had been five years since I had first met them in their Fifth Avenue apartment. I had come to like them. I also had seen from their efforts just how hard it was to give away $40 million.

Charity, as the wealthy conceive of it, has little to do with giving money to someone who asks for it. Most people write checks in response to a solicitation or because they have given to a particular charity for many years. It comes out of a sense of affinity and obligation. According to the annual Giving USA survey, religious and educational organizations rank at the top for donations from people at every income level. Together, they received 45 percent of all donations in 2012. Health and human services organizations do well, too, making up another 21 percent. People support their faith and express gratitude to their alma mater; they are grateful to hospitals and realize that disasters, from floods to distant tsunamis, show how precarious life is. For the wealthy, the dollars are bigger, but so is the pressure to give them away in a manner that makes a difference.

Establishing the thin green line for charity has less to do with a right or a wrong way to give and more with the effectiveness of strategies and what they mean for a person's satisfaction. Chances are they are going to have a plan. According to a Credit Suisse poll of 150 of the world's wealthiest philanthropists, nearly 40 percent consulted a financial adviser and 30 percent talked to their accountant before making a donation; only 23 percent made donations without seeking outside advice. Seventy percent of them said their giving stemmed from a personal vision. But they were still concerned about establishing a professional framework for it: 59 percent of them set up a family foundation to organize their giving. Two-thirds of the respondents said they used a computerized tracking system to measure the impact of their giving. Yet, for some, giving was another business with similar stress: a third felt it was hard to remain engaged in giving away their money—something you would think would be so rewarding and interesting that it would hold their attention.

In a related survey, Credit Suisse found that 18 percent of people with $1 to $5 million in assets were driven by family legacy, but half of those with over $50 million thought about their legacy. Drilling down deeper to what motivates people was more difficult. Some people who were born with far less realize their good fortune and want to give others the chance they had. Some of the less altruistic people have ulterior motives that aren't as bad in charity as they might be in other areas—such as naked social climbing or expiating for past sins. At least money goes to good causes. When it comes to big-time giving, it makes more sense to look at those on the wealthy side of the thin green line as being divided into camps: traditionalists, quants, and members of the pure-joy club.

The Jonases are traditionalists, philanthropists cut from the classic American mold of coming from nothing, making a fortune in business, and then giving it away to a cause they believed would make the world better. The first time I met them, I had to make way for art hangers from the Guggenheim Museum. They were carrying a Pablo Picasso painting around the living room of the Jonases' Central Park apartment. They had lent the museum a Jackson Pollock print that it needed for a show, and the Guggenheim had shuttled over a placeholder. This is one of the perks of having an art collection that museums covet.

When the Jonases sold fifteen pieces of art at a Christie's auction in 2005, it became the basis for the serious philanthropy they decided to undertake in their last years. These were works by the greats of mid-twentieth-century art such as Arshile Gorky, Willem de Kooning, and Mark Rothko. Five of them set auction records, and the sale brought in $44.2 million. They used that money to fund their charitable foundation. "We decided that the art we'd been collecting over thirty years had gone up so much in value that we could do something in philanthropy with it," Mr. Jonas told me shortly after the sale. They had given regularly and generously to many charities, but with the art sale their goal changed: they wanted to make a difference in more people's lives—the stated goal of every big-time philanthropist. They didn't want to write thousands of checks for millions of dollars each year; they wanted to focus on one thing and make it matter.

But the Jonases didn't have an obvious outlet for their largess. They had both grown up poor and had given modestly to Jewish causes throughout their lives. They had done well in business. They didn't have any of the standard guilt or insecurity to assuage with charitable giving. They wanted to do something meaningful. While they were wealthy, it would take billions, not tens of millions, to make a big difference in causes such as poverty and Jewish issues. They had also made their fortune slowly, so unlike tech entrepreneurs who get lucky and make theirs in a blast, they had experienced highs and lows and were not blithely overconfident that what they knew from business would translate into philanthropy. So Mr. Jonas went thematic: he decided to help an underdog who does good and might one day help him. "I always felt nurses and public-school teachers were the most underserved professions," he told me. "Nurses had no real substantial backing." So he started the Jonas Center for Nursing Excellence, figuring he had enough money to improve nursing care in New York. The goal was big enough to occupy his remaining years but also focused, given their resources. They were wealthy, but not hedge-fund titans. Mrs. Jonas added, "We thought, 'Here's a place for us to really make a difference.'"

The Jonases wanted to educate the people who would train the hospital nurses, hoping this would create more and better educators who would in turn produce exponentially more and better nurses in the field. They had done their research and found that a lot of nursing faculty were retiring, so their $44 million could help meet this need. Mr. Jonas commissioned a study in 2010 to find out how many nurses would be affected by their grants. The lead researchers, Darlene Curley, a nurse who was the executive director of the Jonas Center for Nursing Excellence, and Christine Kovner, a PhD in nursing and professor at New York University College of Nursing, came up with a staggering but probably exaggerated number. One nursing professor would "touch the lives" of 3.6 million patients a year over a thirty-year career (based on the number of students a professor teaches over a career and the number of patients a nurse in turn sees in her career). It is hard to believe that the direct impact of one educator would be this high over the three decades a nurse might work. But even if the real number is closer to one-tenth of that, it still showed that their philanthropy would matter.

The Jonases' approach seems simple. They believe giving money to charity is better than having a lot of museum-quality art on their walls. They believe their money can make a difference in a cause, nursing. They went about accomplishing their goal the way many traditionalists have before them. They established a first-rate board of financiers, health-care administrators, doctors, and nurses. Their goal is to fund one thousand Jonas scholars; they were a quarter of the way there when we talked before the golf tournament. But however good their cause, the Jonases have had to go it alone. One of the toughest lessons they learned was that their friends, who had been asking them to donate to their causes for decades, were not so inclined to contribute to their foundation, even if it was helping nurses.

Mr. Jonas said that a few years ago he drew up a list of twelve prominent and wealthy New Yorkers that he knew socially and spent the better part of six months trying to meet with them. He sat down with ten. He wanted them to make sizable donations to his charity through the golf tournament: "They all said, 'Donald, you're doing some great stuff. My foundation doesn't meet for nine months and my company is closed to this sort of thing.' Then they said, 'I'm going to do something personally but don't expect too much.' I knew right then it was five thousand dollars. I was quite disappointed. They could have given untold amounts if they wanted to." Yet, they had their own foundations, boards, and causes to support, and being asked for money did not appeal to them. It's not unique to Mr. Jonas.

According to that Credit Suisse poll, which included Bill Gates, Warren Buffett, and Leon Black, one of the most successful hedge-fund investors in the United States, only 7 percent of the 150 wealthiest philanthropists were willing to partner with another private philanthropist. They preferred to partner with businesses (40 percent), followed by nonprofits and government agencies. All of these civic-minded people were, in essence, stuck in their own charitable silos. "It's a harder sell for these wildly wealthy New York guys," Mr. Jonas said, saddened. "They're overcommitted in what they do."

Pierre Omidyar can certainly go it alone with wealth of nearly $9 billion from founding eBay, the online auction site. If the Jonases represent the traditionalist strand in American philanthropy, the Omidyars are the new cutting edge of giving. Fresher, richer, more data-driven, they are the quants of the philanthropic world. They want to improve entire sectors such as education and create institutions where none existed, and they want to do everything in a precisely measurable way. The Credit Suisse poll, which was skewed to the high-tech sector, found that 44 percent of them wanted to affect change within ten years—a far cry from the days of Carnegie and Rockefeller, whose largess is still being felt. (Only 15 percent thought of their philanthropy as extending beyond their lifetime.)

Their vision may stem from the sort of thing that happened to Omidyar when eBay went public three years after he started it in 1995. Within days of that initial public offering, Omidyar was worth over $1 billion. "I didn't have time to grow overly attached to the fruits of my labor because the labor wasn't that hard," he told me from his home in Honolulu, Hawaii. "I worked really hard for a number of years without a vacation, but it was only three years. I'm very cognizant that it was an inordinate amount of wealth to get in a very short time." Omidyar's mother was a linguist and his father a surgeon. They had emigrated from Iran to Paris for school and then to Washington, DC, when he was six. His family talked little about philanthropy when he was growing up, and he associated giving with responses to disasters. "I wasn't volunteering," he said. "I wasn't making donations. It wasn't an important part of my life—similar to auctions in general or collecting."

The difference between philanthropists such as Donald Jonas and Pierre Omidyar, when it comes to charity, is not in the scale of their wealth but in the time it took to acquire it. That affects the way they give it away. Jonas worked his whole life and was giving away his money toward the end of it. Omidyar, who was thirty-one when eBay went public, said he had seen people work hard for decades building businesses and get nowhere near the kind of wealth he had. He wanted to make sure his vast billions would not be wasted. So several years into giving, he drew a distinction between charity and philanthropy that has served as a guide. Charity meets an immediate need, such as a disaster. Philanthropy, he wrote in a *Harvard Business Review* piece in 2011, was about a way "to improve the state of humanity and the world"—to make things better tomorrow.

This desire, he told me, came from seeing how eBay ended up functioning. It allowed people to buy and sell things, but it also helped them build the trust among strangers necessary for the transactions to take place. He wanted his philanthropy to function in the same way: "I didn't want to promote a type of philanthropy that was about my own interests. I wanted to help others meet their own goals, the same way as the eBay platform." Omidyar decided to combine philanthropy, which doesn't have to be paid back, and private equity investment, which does. His idea, at the time, was novel; no one else was doing it his way. Microlending was one thing he invested money in. "Supporting a small entrepreneur in India so he can make loans to someone at the base of the pyramid [philanthrospeak for "the poor-est of the poor"], that's private equity, but it's really philanthropy," Omidyar explained. "If you just gave that person a grant, then he wouldn't have the motivation and market feedback to build a self-sustaining enterprise. He'd just come back for another grant." While microlending has been marred by scandals over high interest rates, it embodies the notion of social change embedded in what Omidyar and others are trying to do.

When we spoke, his Omidyar Network, which houses his grant-making and investment arms, was focused on education and mobile technologies to improve the lives of people in the develop-ing world. One of its projects is Bridge International Academies, a Kenyan organization that quickly and relatively inexpensively builds a "school in a box" in poor rural areas. In 2009, the Omidyar Net-work invested $1.8 million and the group built over eighty schools, each one educating some three hundred children at a tuition of $4 per month. The goal is for this concept to spread throughout Africa and to other parts of the developing world. In philanthrospeak, the concept is scalable, meaning it can be replicated anywhere. But this school also shows a big weakness or at least a limitation to Omidyar's approach. Many of these so-called impact philanthropists are not tackling equivalent issues in the developed world, such as education reform, income inequality, or quality nursing care. In poor countries, their dollars can have a far greater impact since people are starting from a much lower point. "If you can build a school in the slums of Nairobi for forty thousand dollars, you can only renovate a bathroom in a US school for forty thousand dollars," Omidyar admitted. "My passion is really about the developing world because of the potential to impact hundreds of thousands of people with reasonable sums." Or as the managing partner of the Omidyar Network, Matt Bannick, told me at the Clinton Global Initiative in

New York, "People tell us, 'It's great you're working on education in the developing world, but we have our problems here.' The question for us is 'How do we engage in a way that is catalytic?' Opening a few new charter schools isn't going to cut it."

Combining what he has already done and plans to do over the next fifty years, Omidyar could greatly improve life in the poorest parts of the world. People such as him might not help narrow the gap between the One Percent and the 99 percent in the United States, but they could narrow the gap between the poor in Africa and the poor in the United States, who seem as rich as the One Percent from the third world. "Our role as philanthropists is to understand the greatest need and the greatest potential to have impact to lift people out of poverty and to insure human dignity," Omidyar told me. "There is a natural compassion that exists in people. Technology has driven down the cost of interventions and increased the desire to help others. We're in a period of time where as humanity we'll be better positioned to address the problems we have."

Paul Piff, a psychologist at the University of California, Berkeley, has less charitable views about wealthy philanthropists. He thinks they're cheap, look too far away to find people to help, or some combination of the two. He has come up with some novel studies to test his hypotheses and to measure the relative compassion and willingness to be charitable between wealthier and poorer people. The experiments aim to evaluate how social class influences people's sense of community, moral judgment, and generosity. His conclusions show wealthier people favoring money over community. This shocked him. But it made perfect sense to me. If you have a lot of money, you don't need to ask your friends to help you do things: you can pay people to do those things for you. His studies, though, delve into the crux of giving: Should we help only those we know, more in the Jonas mold, or should we aim for a greater good, as Omidyar does, even if it comes at the expense of things closer to home that also need fixing?

Piff punts on that issue. His interest is more in the psychological motivations that get people to write the check. The first reason people give, he said, is that other people are giving, and it reflects well on them. He equated it to affluent people who buy a Toyota Prius, which is twice the price of a regular Toyota and just as uncomfortable. But because it is a hybrid, it makes them look good in certain circles in a way that a Mercedes-Benz C-Class, which is about the same price as a Prius and nicer in every way but fuel efficiency and eco-smugness, would not. "Philanthropy showcases their altruism," he told me. "Giving money to an alma mater shows you're a generous person. You're getting reputational benefits as the result." That's not a bad reason. Mrs. Jonas said she felt that before they focused on nursing they were subject to "social blackmail"—friends and acquaintances asked them to give to their charities and would give the same to the Jonases'. But there was no coherent plan: it was just giving to causes and going to dinners, which is how most people with a bit of money to spare do it.

The second reason for giving, Piff found, was that people, after rising to the top of their profession, could see how tough it was to get there and might even admit their ascent was the result of luck as much as skill. The more empathetic among them want to do something to help others in a challenging and unfair world.

The risk for people in need is that it is becoming more compelling among the wealthiest today—think the Silicon Valley elite—to try to eradicate malaria in Africa, which is a logistically difficult but medically simple problem, than it is to end hunger in America or improve a public school system full of poor kids and absent or overworked parents. Twenty-seven percent of philanthropists with more than $50 million are focusing their giving internationally, the Credit Suisse survey found. Piff had a different take on this. Whether in Africa or inner-city America, the donors could be dispassionate about problems that inspire passion and look at a broader segment of society than just their neighbors. "The idea that richer people make more utilitarian decisions because of their reduced compassion is hard," Piff said. "But there's a positive twist to not feeling the suffering of another person when you need to make that choice: in certain kinds of situations, wealthier people were more able to balance the costs and the benefits because they were less sensitive to the suffering of one person versus many."

But why wouldn't you help your neighbor? Piff found that people who felt wealthier than someone else, regardless of their actual wealth, care less about their neighbor. In several different studies, Piff manipulated his subjects so that they felt wealthier or poorer than they actually were; they behaved differently. "Intuitively it would seem that you'd have to be different if you were born wealthy versus becoming wealthy yourself," Piff said. His experiments prove otherwise. "If I bring wealthier people into the lab and make them feel poor, they behave more ethically." In one example, they took fewer pieces of candy reserved for children. In another they were less likely to cheat. Piff said that in a separate study he asked participants to write down three ways that working collaboratively is better. When they took the test, they scored higher on these measures than the group that had not been asked to think about collaboration before being tested. In another study, which sought to look at people's willingness to volunteer their time, wealthy people who watched a forty-six-second video on childhood poverty were measurably more receptive to a request to stay later and help someone they did not know than the people who did not watch the video. And the converse: people who made $10 an hour who were made to feel wealthier than the person asking for help suddenly felt that their time was worth more and did not stay longer to help the stranger. "There is a lot of malleability to this stuff," Piff said. "Wealth or poverty endows the individual with certain types of social environments. They exert these patterned effects on others. If you're wealthier, you're more cut off. You think of yourself as bigger. You use more resources. But if you reverse this, you can flip the whole thing."

Piff's studies only go so far. He is testing people in a wide but not complete band of wealth. He said he has been unable to study people who were really poor—making less than $15,000 a year—and those who were above the top 3 percent in America, which would be about $200,000 a year. Still, he said, "The most robust determinant of behavior is how you're feeling right now." His studies do not mean that wealthy people are not responding to calls for help at a generous rate. They are. They are also more forward-looking in how they think about the effect of money given in a noncrisis situation, instead of just responding to a request. This mind-set means that they are looking dispassionately at a need and assessing it. Do they give a neighbor who has made some bad financial choices $1,000 to rectify them, or do they donate $1,000 to a relief effort in a place such as Haiti where the same amount of money will help dozens of people? The rational choice is obvious, but it is not going to make the neighbor happy. Just as Fertel thought when his father turned down his request for a bailout on his visit to Zurich, the neighbor is going to think his wealthy friend has the means but is choosing to be cheap. Instead, the wealthy person may be thinking that he is maximizing his charitable dollars—or that his neighbor is a spendthrift who makes bad choices. For the less wealthy, the desire to help a neighbor can have negative economic consequences and limit their ability to improve their current circumstances. "They'll embed themselves in these communities that help them get by but do not show them how to get ahead," Piff said. "When the economic times are literally tough, wealthier people want to maximize personal achievement. It's a question of what do you value."

The terms *wealthier* and *community* are always relative. As I wrote in the chapter on debt, with the overleveraged people of Darien, Connecticut, some of the people in these communities are affluent by any measure, but they may not be as wealthy as the family with the home on the water. This perception may make them more community minded in their giving but less able to imagine a world beyond the perfect town where they live. "Resources matter a lot, but the subjective sense of wealth matters more," Piff said. "The more money you make, the more educated you are, the higher you place yourself on the ladder. There is a distinction between where you stand and where you think you stand."

This distinction was one of the dynamics at work in the Occupy Wall Street protests in New York. Those siding with the OWS movement, according to David Graeber, an anthropologist and one of the movement's initial organizers, were overwhelmingly young, educated, and affluent by most standards. If not all as well educated and wealthy as Sobel, they could still take time off from school or work—or not work with their parents' help—to participate in protests against an economic system they deemed unfair. They may have been saddled with college-loan debt, but no one had forced them to go to an expensive private college over a less expensive state university or to live afterward in an expensive city such as New York. (To me, the most incongruous OWS encampment I saw was the one across from the main gate at Yale University, where Ivy League students shouted OWS slogans, iPhones and iPads all around.) Yet, this group of comparatively privileged protesters was battling people who lived in the nicest neighborhoods of Manhattan and Brooklyn or the Westchester and Fairfield County suburbs.

The counterargument of people in these nice neighborhoods

was equally fraught: they were not rich because it cost a lot to live and raise children where they did, and they shouldn't be demonized for their success. While that was certainly true, they were rich in the eyes of the nation. Complaining about the carrying costs on a $2 million house or the high costs of private school do not make you a sympathetic figure to most of America—even if your neighbor has a larger house and more children in private school. "It's the perceptions of what you have," Piff said, "that enacts these behaviors all the way down the ladder." Those perceptions influence people's inclinations to help someone less fortunate than them or to hold on to their money because they have less than their wealthier neighbor.

All of this is predicated on the belief that giving your money to the less fortunate is a good thing. While it would be seen by many as selfish to hoard your fortune to protect your children, it could also be seen as a rational decision. Not all wealthy people feel the need to give to charity. Larry Ellison, the founder of Oracle, the software company, and one of the twenty richest people in the world, had a long history of being uncharitable until he signed Bill Gates' and Warren Buffett's Giving Pledge in 2010. Ellison released a statement when he signed it saying he had put 95 percent of his assets in trust and had always planned to give them away quietly. Perhaps that was his intent all along, but given his extravagant lifestyle—from sponsoring America's Cup sailing teams to buying an island in Hawaii to cycling through wives—his critics were skeptical. It once seemed that he had been pressured into giving $115 million to Harvard University—even though he had never attended it and dropped out of two colleges in Illinois—until he rescinded the pledge. (He said he changed his mind after Larry Summers left the Harvard presidency.) Carlos Slim Helú, the Mexican telecommunications mogul and the only man in the world richer than Bill Gates, had a more nuanced view on not being charitable. "The only way to fight poverty is with employment," he said according to a *Wall Street Journal* report. "Trillions of dollars have been given to charity in the last fifty years, and they don't solve anything." He added that he had no intention of signing the Giving Pledge. "There is a saying that we should leave a better country to our children," he said. "But it's more important to leave better children to our country." Slim is not a miser, though: he funds ventures that look to create jobs for poor people.

Most wealthy people who are charitable are motivated by the intrinsic reward of doing a good thing or the social cachet gained from being on the boards and at the events that come with being philanthropic. Charles Bronfman, the former cochairman of the Seagram Company and founder of the Andrea and Charles Bronfman Philanthropies, told me that he never felt pressure to donate. "I never give back," he said. "I don't like that term. I give because I want to give." Bronfman, who wrote two books on philanthropy—*The Art of Giving* and *The Art of Doing Good*—said the philanthropic engine in America was constant. Even when the economy was bad, he said, giving never dipped as far as the economy, and it returned at the leading edge of any recovery. "It can be for guilt; it can be for pleasure; but at the end of the day, giving is something that makes you feel better," he told me.

Bank of America's "Study of High Net Worth Philanthropy" found in 2012 that 95 percent of high-net-worth households—defined as people with a net worth greater than $1 million or more than $200,000 a year in earnings—gave to charity as compared with 65 percent of the general population. Furthermore, the top 3 percent of high-net-worth households gave half of the $300 billion donated to charity the year before. This group gave away about 9 percent of their income. They also volunteered in droves—88 percent of them—with most of that time going to serving on nonprofit boards. The study found that "wealthy donors give at the greatest rates under the following circumstances: being moved by how a gift can make a difference (74 percent), feeling financially secure (71 percent), because they give to the same organization or cause annually (69 percent), and because they feel the organization they are supporting is efficient (68 percent)." Less than a third, the study said, gave for tax reasons, and half said they would keep giving even if the charitable tax deduction were eliminated. Among the richest, 95 percent said they would keep giving to charity even if the estate tax were repealed. Only 18 percent went on the record as saying that they felt "the need for visibility or recognition based on these activities." This data might seem to contradict Piff's studies but it reinforces them: these donors are making reasoned choices about whom to give to—not missing work to help a neighbor fix a busted water pipe. This is where being on the right side of the thin green line can be good for the broader population but can cause resentment or misunderstanding among needy people closer to the donor.

Most of us who are not multimillionaires or billionaires give money to charity because we believe in the cause or the act itself makes us feel good. This gets derided as checkbook philanthropy by advisers who help the wealthiest. But some people among the wealthiest in the world act the same way. They're members of what I call the pure-joy club. Their mix of planning and spontaneity can serve as a model to others because it can be adapted by people with far less money. One in this third school—albeit with plenty of wealth—is Jon Huntsman Sr., among the most generous people in the world that most people don't know of. He is one of only a handful of philanthropists ever to give away more than $1 billion.

Despite that level of giving, he is moved the way an average person might be. At the end of 1988, for example, Huntsman was watching television at his home in Utah. All the news coverage was about a devastating earthquake in Armenia, which was then part of the Soviet Union. Some sixty thousand people were killed and hundreds of thousands were left homeless; 80 percent of the buildings in the city of Spitak crumbled. "I didn't know where it was," Huntsman told me. "It just got to my heart. You saw these families who were destroyed." He wanted to help, and so he did, getting on a plane to Armenia with Armand Hammer, a doctor and businessman who once controlled Occidental Petroleum. Huntsman has since visited the country forty-six times and given $50 million to help rebuild it. Each year, he sponsors a couple of dozen Armenian students to come to the United States to study. "I don't know what took hold of me," he said. "Or why I gave. It's hard to know what goes on inside your head."

The son of a strict and at times abusive rural schoolteacher in Idaho, Huntsman, a Mormon, was given a scholarship by a Jewish family in San Francisco to attend the University of Pennsylvania. He made the most of it. "I knew I was lucky," he said. "I could have never done that on my own." He never forgot that chance. Starting out selling eggs after getting out of the Navy, Huntsman got into manufacturing. In 1974, he invented the clamshell box for the McDonald's Big Mac. He sold his company, Huntsman Container Corporation, two years later and got into polystyrene, a little-loved-but-much-used plastic. It's what packing peanuts, disposable razors, and yogurt cups are made of. Huntsman took his company, Huntsman Chemical Corporation, and expanded it into a manufacturer of everything from specialty textiles to the carbon-fiber chassis on the Lamborghini Aventador. Annual revenue in 2013 was $12 billion, he said.

But his giving started early. He was a young Navy officer, earning $320 a month, and giving above his tithing to the Church of Jesus Christ of Latter-day Saints to groups that helped people in need.

"Looking back on it, we probably needed that three hundred and twenty dollars a month," he said. But he was hooked on the joy it gave him. Huntsman, who was seventy-six when we spoke, said that by the time he made his first $1 million in business, he and his wife, Karen, had given away between 20 and 25 percent of it. Their goal was simply to help, writing checks to a range of groups, from charities to help the homeless to the local symphony. As his wealth grew, so did the sums, though he considers them small in comparison to today's. "We found that we were giving to thirty or forty different charities, between ten thousand and fifty thousand dollars," he said. "Maybe one of them got two and a half million dollars." He said he wouldn't know how much he had given away if *Forbes* magazine hadn't estimated it. He took their number, then a few years old, and added recent donations to put it at about $1.6 billion in 2013. The sums, he said, don't matter to him; it's the commitment to a cause. His biggest one has been the Huntsman Cancer Institute in Utah. He has given $450 million to it and set the bold goal of curing cancer. He has a personal connection, having survived four bouts of the disease, which claimed the lives of his mother, father, and stepmother. "If someone said, 'Jon, we need two hundred and fifty million dollars a year from now and we can make a dramatic breakthrough for ovarian cancer,' I'd have two hundred and fifty million dollars in two months," he told me. "You just work day and night if the cause in your heart is justified. You just go out and drive yourself to get the money. And you have fun doing it. It's a real rush. It's also very emotional for me."

Not surprisingly he has no patience for people who don't give to charity. While he was in the first group to sign the Buffett-Gates Giving Pledge, he said he thinks the notion of giving away just half is silly: "My suggestion was to give eighty percent away. Why do they need half of ten billion dollars to live on?" When it comes to using his considerable business skill to run the hospital that bares his name, he didn't see any point in trying: "I just slip the check under the door and run for cover. They know what they're doing and I don't." That's a rare thing for a billionaire to say at a time when so many believe success in one business gives them a particular insight into how philanthropy could work more efficiently if only they were involved.

Yet Huntsman is not constrained by giving plans or the glamour of big donations. He told me he was in a restaurant and struck up a conversation with the waiter, who was a Cuban immigrant. The man said he was getting married and was working to put himself through college. "I said, 'Give me your name and address,' and I'm sending him through college. I'm excited and enthused by the opportunity to give." Nor is he bothered when he is targeted for handouts. At the hotel in Philadelphia where he stays, he is known for giving anyone who helps him $100. On a visit shortly before we spoke, he said the bellman who takes care of him—for good reason—wasn't there. "I was in my room and I heard this knock on the door. I opened it and there was Daniel. He said, 'I brought up some extra bottles of water for you.' I said, 'I knew when I walked in that you weren't here. Here's your hundred dollars.'" This is not the type of planned giving or philanthropy with a cause that any adviser would advocate, but it brings Huntsman satisfaction. "It's a type of enjoyment. The joy is not necessarily in getting the accolades from doing it. We're not in the movie business. We don't make a rule of putting out how much we give. We just love the thrill of watching these people where something has happened in their life."

Huntsman does not care about philanthropic advisers or metrics to measure the success of his giving either. He simply expects the cancer researchers to show progress, just as he expects students who received scholarships to get good grades and the battered women who were given shelter through another charity to have the chance to start a new life. "It's not the amount you give," he said, "but that you give."

Giving away your money, one scholar argues, can also help you financially. Arthur Brooks, president of the American Enterprise In-stitute, analyzed data on thirty thousand American households and found that people who gave to charity were generally more affluent, all other things being equal. (He also found that Utah was the most charitable state in America.) "If you have two families that are exactly identical—in other words, same religion, same race, same number of kids, same town, same level of education, and everything's the same—except that one family gives a hundred dollars more to charity than the second family, then the giving family will earn on average three hundred and seventy-five dollars more in income than the nongiving family," he said in a speech in 2009. People who volunteer also do bet-ter financially, the data showed. Brooks said he doubted this finding could be true at first. Then he saw data showing how growth in giving had outpaced purchasing power by 40 percentage points in the fifty years leading up to 2004. It was, he found, a case of the two pushing and pulling each other. It was also linked to what psychologists had been studying for years—the connection between happiness and gen-erosity. "People who give to charity are forty-three percent more likely than people who don't give to say they're very happy people," Brooks said. "People who give blood are twice as likely to say they're very happy people as people who don't give blood. People who volunteer are happier. The list goes on. You simply can't find any kind of ser-vice that won't make you happier." Now, what's harder to determine is if happier people are more naturally charitable: Could a miserable curmudgeon become a decent dinner companion by giving more to charity? The key, he said, was that giving and volunteering lowered people's stress levels, and that had a positive effect in other areas of their lives, such as earning a living. It also allowed others to see them as leaders, which helped them rise in their profession.

———————

Six years after Mrs. Jonas and her husband sold half of their paintings to fund their charitable work, she still misses them. On my last meeting in their apartment, she took me to a back room to show me a photo of 250 Jonas scholars in nursing, a collection of men and women of different ages and races. "They're from all over the place," she said. "They're black, white, men, women, all sizes and shapes, and they're everywhere." But in the corner, in inexpensive frames you would have bought at Lechters, were snapshots of her paintings that had been sold to start the foundation. They weren't professionally shot but snapped before the art was taken off to auction. "This is where I cry," she said. "This is a particularly exciting de Kooning. A Pollock. A Motherwell. These were all things Donald wanted to sell, but I didn't. There was a lot of sadness." She paused. "He said we'd lived with these for thirty-five years—it's time for us to give back. I said, 'After our death we'll give back.' These were my children. We didn't buy them to sell them. We compromised after many tears: we sold fifteen and kept fifteen."

As we walked back to the front room, Mr. Jonas was quiet. He knew it had been hard for his wife to agree to sell the paintings. But she had come around and was clearly proud of the people their money was helping. "I can see that it's changed our life immeasurably," she said. "He would be a very unhappy soul if we hadn't done this. He would be sitting here looking at the paintings and be very unhappy."

No matter how much someone gives, a bit of pain for the donor is a good thing: it reminds the giver that he or she is sacrificing something. It may also help the person connect, even a bit, with people at different points on the thin green line.

THINK ABOUT IT AGAIN

9

MONEY CAUSES STRESS FOR EVERYONE

I felt calm as I sat on a blue couch and joked with Joel Reimer, a fit, fiftysomething man in a golf shirt. He was putting electrical sensors on my thumb and fingers. I was in the middle of Kansas, sitting in one of the exam rooms at the Financial Therapy Clinic, a counseling and research center run by the Institute of Personal Financial Planning at Kansas State University. The clinic was on Poyntz Avenue, the main street in Manhattan, Kansas, in a building full of small businesses in small offices. The office, like the town, the street, and the building, was clean, spare, and quiet. I couldn't tell if the town had once been bigger and bustling or if this was as it had always been, empty until game day, when alumni and visiting teams came to K-State for Big 12 football and basketball games.

"So I appreciate you coming in today," Reimer said. "I'm just going to ask you some questions. Some background questions first and some financial goal-setting questions. Do you have any questions?"

I didn't. He began by asking about my marital status, children, and employment status. Then he went into questions about my finances and about the goals we had. *Which of the following best describes your financial situation at the end of the month: Do you have several unpaid bills, do you break even, or do you have some money left over?* We had money left over, I said. *Suppose you were to sell all of your possessions, including your home, so you have turned all your assets into cash and you were going to pay off your debt. After paying off that debt, would you be in serious debt, break even, or have a lot of money left over?* I asked him what he meant by a lot since that was a relative term. He wouldn't say, but I chose it anyway since we would have money left. Then came some questions to rate my satisfaction with our adviser and stress levels around money. I said very satisfied with my adviser and not particularly stressed about our financial situation. I gave myself high marks on financial literacy, and a moderate grade for my willingness to take a risk on an investment.

The most thought-provoking questions centered on our three financial goals for the year. I was sure I would shine on these. My wife and I had given a lot of thought to how much we were spending and saving in the year since I had sat down with Tiger 21 members. We had taken the time to do all those things most people don't bother to do until much later, from creating a financial plan to buying insurance to writing wills and selecting a guardian for our children. Our goals, I figured, were minor: we were trying to figure out how much to set aside for college savings now so it would have time to grow when we needed it later. We wanted to determine how much of our disposable income should go into a brokerage account and how much to paying down the principal on our mortgage. One of my three goals was to go on a couple of trips in the coming year since we had been so frugal since the financial crash. "That's it for our questions at this point," said Reimer with the same friendly but unreadable expression he had had since the start. "We'll let you go on out and answer some additional questions." He unhooked me from the machine.

If anything, the written questions should have been easier because they were focused entirely on basic financial concepts, responsibilities, and anxieties around money. But the last section caused me to pause. The questions were straightforward, but they asked for actual numbers, such as what were our monthly housing costs and income after taxes? I had been honest up to this point. But I didn't want to reveal this information, even though Reimer was a complete stranger and I didn't know anyone in Manhattan, Kansas. My concern was what someone else would think: I didn't want Reimer or whoever else read my answers to think I was a jerk or, worse, a rich jerk. Our monthly expenses were, if anything, moderate compared to our income and where we lived. But they would be considered high or unbelievably high here in the Little Apple, as the chamber of commerce had dubbed Manhattan, Kansas. So I lied, underestimating both.

I shouldn't have bothered, I soon found out. The researchers didn't care about any of my answers. They did not care about my level of financial knowledge. They had been testing my stress levels around talking about money.

"Do you think you were stressed or not stressed?" Sonya Britt, the chair of the Institute of Personal Financial Planning at K-State, asked me. She had been watching a video of me answering Reimer and monitoring the sensors on my fingers.

"I don't think I was stressed," I said. "I think I was cold."

"Hmmm . . . you actually were quite stressed. It doesn't matter what the room temperature is. After about two minutes, you should be able to adjust and go back to your homeostasis level. You got more stressed as you went on."

She then showed me a graph of temperature at my fingertips. It started at seventy-four degrees and dropped to seventy-two during the questioning. The ideal temperature, she said, was ninety-two degrees. Most people who were relaxed were around eighty-two or higher.

"This has nothing to do with the temperature of the room?" I asked.

"No. What's happening in that situation is your blood is going back to your heart. It's the fight-or-flight response. There's not blood left in your fingers."

As if that were not bad enough, she added that my "skin conducent level"—science-speak for sweaty fingers—doubled during questioning. I was cold *and* clammy.

"The purpose of that experiment was to see how people reacted to talking to a financial adviser," said Britt. "It is stressful. And it's more stressful having to answer questions about your goals, which is not that surprising." I wanted to know about our twenty minutes of questions: What were they supposed to tell her? "We don't actually use them for anything," she said. So were my answers irrelevant? "Yes."

After all I had learned from Tiger 21 and writing this book, I had failed the test. She was kinder: I had finished at the bottom of the sample—meaning despite a far greater knowledge of finance than most people and a solid financial situation personally, I had done worse than people just walking in off the street knowing nothing. Far from dispiriting, the results fascinated me: I knew the pitfalls of poor planning and how it can ruin anyone's life plans. I had worked hard to get our finances in order. But talking about money was still stressful—even to complete strangers.

The researchers at Kansas State's Institute of Personal Financial Planning have been doing interesting work into how people think and feel about money through tests such as the one I took. With them, they are able to determine how the body reacts, no matter what the mouth says. As I sat there, if I had answered the questions again, knowing what I now knew, I doubted I could have masked my stress any better. It made perfect sense to me why I was so stressed and also why getting on the right side of the thin green line can be so tough. It takes an openness and honesty that is hard to muster, even around complete strangers.

"My stress isn't 'I'm not going to be able to pay my bills,'" I said. "My stress is 'I know how people perceive money.' It was more stressful filling out the money parts of this survey."

"Just divulging the numbers," Reimer said.

"Exactly," I said, nodding in relief.

As I was leaving, I asked Britt who had the lowest stress level in this experiment. She turned to Reimer, and they agreed it was a chatty teacher. "Basically she had never talked to anyone about her finances before and she wanted to keep talking," Britt said. "We felt bad that we had to move her along." The teacher didn't know what she didn't know or should worry about. She just knew that she had a pension at the end of her teaching career and that she had saved some money, too. I'd bet she was probably wealthy and on the safe side of the thin green line.

I had learned about the studies being done in Manhattan, Kansas, from Brad Klontz, whom I introduced in chapter 2. His research focuses on money disorders, and I thought he and his colleagues at Kansas State were doing some of the most interesting research I had seen into how people developed their "money scripts"—the stories they told themselves about what money meant in their lives. Two years after the financial meltdown of 2008, he had surveyed a group of people about seventy-two money-related beliefs and found that most people fell into four broad categories—money avoidance, money worship, money status, and money vigilance. Each had its own complications. People with money avoidance, somewhat simply, tried to distance themselves from money, often thinking that they did not deserve it. The result was predictable: they undermined their financial well-being. Those who worshipped money believed it would cure all their problems. If they only had more money, their thinking went, everything that was wrong with their lives would be solved. People with a money status script seemed similar to money worshippers except that they connected money to their sense of well-being. Or, as Klontz put it, their self-worth was linked to their net worth. The last script was money vigilance. These people did not flaunt what they had, paid their debts on time, and were generally cautious about overspending. If anything, they were the ones who could deprive themselves for no reason. "We need to identify the set of beliefs that work and the ones that don't and modify them or let go of them," he told me when this study came out in 2011.

A follow-up study tested respondents for what Klontz and Britt, his coauthor on several of these papers, called "disordered money behaviors." They listed these as "compulsive buying, pathological gambling, compulsive hoarding, workaholism, financial enabling, financial dependence, financial denial, and financial enmeshment." The study aimed to look deeper than the research on how mastering the basics of finance—such as keeping track of expenses—affected people. It tracked measures of people's agreement or disagreement with pathological money behaviors that would have far worse effects on people than whether they balanced their checkbook. One goal in naming these behaviors was to help financial advisers identify them, since they were more likely to encounter them than mental health professionals. A third study by Klontz and Britt brought much of their research together and laid it out in a practical way for advisers. Their hope, in all of this research, was to create awareness that would lead to advisers helping clients to think better about money. "Once identified," they wrote, "money scripts can be challenged and changed to interrupt destructive financial patterns and promote financial health."

Like other mental health problems, these money scripts often existed outside of people's consciousness and were formed in reaction to events in their lives. Klontz said those reactions, not the events themselves, mattered most. One example he gave me was of a family on the verge of losing its house because of some bad decisions it had made. In one case, a grandparent comes in and saves the family. In another, the parents scramble and save the house themselves. In a third, they lose it. The precipitating event was the same in all three cases, but how those people will feel about money will be quite different. Those perceptions were what made helping people overcome their money disorders so difficult for advisers. Klontz's own grandfather had suffered from a money script, born out of the Great Depression, that said all banks were bad and could not be trusted. He never put any money in a bank or an investment. "The problem with money scripts is they are always one hundred percent true in a certain context," Klontz told me. "However, since that experience was so emotionally intense, any sort of disconfirming evidence he saw through his life he totally ignored. The federal government came in and guaranteed deposits. It didn't matter. You still can't trust banks." When his grandfather died, Klontz was going through his stuff in the attic and found piles of money. "Behavioral finance has done a lot of research on how memory works and what is typical for human beings interacting around money," Klontz said. "What it lacks is a focus on personal issues and personal differences. How does your history lead to your thoughts and behaviors?" In his grandfather's case no amount of contradictory evidence could sway him to thinking banks were anything but corrupt. For anyone who wants to live on the right side of the thin green line, seeking out that contradictory evidence, accepting it, and applying it is crucial.

In the studies Klontz and I undertook, we looked to tread on both sides of the thin green line by comparing affluent people with people most would consider rich, even if they were not wealthy. We wanted to know if there were any statistically significant differences in behaviors around money. Would you think like a wealthy person if you were in the One Percent and like a rich person if you were just outside of it? Or would both have admirable financial behaviors given their wealth compared to the rest of America? It wasn't this cut-and-dried. In their ways of thinking about money, the One Percent were better off. They were less likely to sabotage their financial success by overspending, gambling away their money, or failing to stick to a budget—all classic traits of money avoidance. They were savers. If anything they worried about not having enough money. They would tell friends that they made less than they did. They equated financial success with a desire to make more money—and focused on that goal. This showed they had money vigilance and a coterie of advisers. They were significantly less likely to mow their own lawn, but they still cooked for themselves: less than 5 percent had a personal chef. Yet as a percentage of their income, they spent about the same on their home as everyone else—23 percent versus 21 percent. The One Percent did drive nicer cars, wear nicer watches, and spend more on vacations. They were also generally happier about life and their prospects for the future. Few of these findings would come as a surprise, particularly to those inclined to believe that happiness and wealth are correlated.

Two things were significantly different about the One Percent that helped put them on the right side of the thin green line. They had what Klontz termed an "internal locus of control." This meant they believed they were in charge of what happened in their lives, good or bad, and if it was bad, they could fix it. They were not at the whim of external forces that controlled their lives, truthfully or not. This internal locus of control meant they took more credit for the success they had in life and personal responsibility for their failures. Beyond being a healthier way to think about their lives, this state of mind meant they were less likely to repeat their mistakes. That's crucial. It is so often not one mistake but one mistake after another that puts people on the wrong side of the thin green line. The second area of difference was with their aversion to losses in their investments. As I pointed out in chapter 2, they make the same foolish mistakes as everyone else when it comes to investing money. But they did not let those losses linger in their portfolios. They were okay with selling the investment at a loss and not hoping the investment would rebound over time. In this, they could also avoid greater losses if that investment continued heading down and put that money into a new investment. They took more control. They accepted contradictory information.

The next morning, I was back in the Financial Therapy Clinic with Klontz and Britt. At the end of my research, I wanted a more rigorous assessment of my own psychology around money. I wanted two financial psychologists to assess me the way a group of wealthy men had at Tiger 21. I wanted to see how well I could accept contradictory evidence. I wanted to know if I could accept it better than most. That kind of acceptance, of things that contradict what you believe should happen, is a key to being on the right side of the thin green line.

As I sat down, Klontz stood in front of me with a tape measure dangling from one hand and a pair of scissors in the other.

"How long do men generally live in your family?" he asked.

"I had one grandfather who died at eighty-six and another at sixty-five, of cancer," I said. "My grandmothers both lived to be over ninety."

"Let's be optimistic."

"Okay, eighty."

"Eighty's optimistic? Let's go for eighty-five."

He cut the tape measure at eighty-five inches. "How old are you now?"

"Thirty-nine."

He snipped the tape at thirty-nine and said, "All gone. This is what we have left."

"Jesus Christ," I gasped.

"This is a very visceral experience you're having now."

It sure was. My mouth went dry, and I felt my stomach drop. It was a parlor trick, but one that drove home a point about focusing on the decisions that I could control going forward and to forget about ones in the past.

"Now when do you want to retire?" he asked.

"Seventy."

"Okay, we have from here to here to get you there."

Looking at that thirty-one inches of working, saving, and being with my family ahead of me felt okay. Seeing those fifteen inches of life that remained when I stopped working felt awful. Klontz knew that my money script was vigilance. This meant I wouldn't overspend and go broke, but my fear of struggling with money like my parents had meant I might also not spend enough to enjoy life. Seeing the horror on my face, he said, "I'd hate for you to sacrifice everything for this here at the end. You don't want to give away this much of your life for this, which is so small. Are you going to be so vigilant that you're not going to be able to travel with your family?"

Far different from the questions that launched this book after I left a mansion on the Upper East Side of New York in a daze. There, a bunch of wealthy men told me all the things my wife and I were doing wrong with our money, and I felt despondent. Here with

Klontz, it felt pretty raw. Still I wanted Klontz and Britt to tell me how I was thinking about money on a deeper level than I understood when I answered their questions the day before. It was easy to sell a second home, as Tiger 21 had advised me to do, but it was hard to change how you think about money. Thinking correctly or incorrectly about money was going to drive how key decisions were made. It was the most important thing I could work on. What did my financial situation mean to me? Am I happier with more money? Was I on the right side of the thin green line or just managing costs and expenses better? I hoped I had moved across it, but I wasn't sure.

"How would you describe your relationship with money?" Klontz asked.

"I'd like to think I have a fairly neutral view of it. I'd rather have more than less. I like to pay off all of our bills every month. I don't like to have any debt beyond a mortgage."

He wanted to know why. I told him about the stories I had heard about my parents and debt. I told him how I associated their arguments when I was a child with their lack of money. Debt to me, particularly credit-card debt, was a façade—why buy something if it was going to sit on a credit card and end up costing much more when the interest was factored in? He wanted to know how old I was when I realized "something weird is going on here" with money. As soon as I was old enough to realize anything, I thought. "I was deeply aware of it as a kid," I told him. I remembered the arguments my parents had over the weekly child-support check, which in retrospect were futile. My father paid $85 a week and it was supposed to arrive on Friday; instead he mailed it on Friday and it arrived on Monday or Tuesday, which would prompt my mother to call him on Saturday and yell at him. "It took me years to wonder, why didn't my mother adjust her expectations and plan for the check to arrive on Tuesday? She could have saved herself all the yelling and screaming. But that was part of it." The *it* was their divorce, which they were as bad at as their marriage.

"What sort of conclusions did you come up with around money as a child?" Klontz asked.

This was the heart of the matter, something I hadn't thought about for the better part of a decade. "I didn't want it. I thought money was bad. I thought it would cause problems. I remember getting my first job at twenty-two. I didn't want to talk about the salary. I played it off. The next job, I said something stupid, like money doesn't matter. I didn't want to squabble over money. I didn't want to ask for more the way a normal person would negotiate for a job."

"What changed?"

"I was very vigilant," I said, not answering his question. "I always knew exactly how much I had charged on my credit cards each month. When I was in my twenties, I knew I couldn't spend more than twelve hundred dollars on my credit card. The four-week months, it was three hundred dollars a week. The five-week months were tough. I thought about it around dates and things I'd buy. It was very unhealthy. But if I was one hundred dollars below the limit, I'd splurge that month." This was mental accounting before I had ever heard the term. Yet this spending plan precluded extra savings beyond what I was contributing through work: I'd spend to my budget, no more or no less.

"Interpersonally you didn't want to touch the topic of money, but at the same time you were deeply concerned about where it was going?"

Exactly, I thought. "At Bloomberg I got a sense of money. I started to know my value as a journalist. I got better at negotiating for myself." I would also go on vacations. I wasn't depriving myself. I was practicing inflexible budgeting. I told him what changed was when I wrote a few longer freelance pieces that paid well and gave me a cushion. I was able to relax, a bit. That level of comfort grew but only so much. I still get no joy out of buying things I don't need. I hate to waste anything.

"What do you think about your internal sense of comfort around your wife spending money versus you spending money?" Klontz asked.

"I don't really like spending. I don't feel like I need any more. I wouldn't have any trouble going out and buying an Apple computer whatever it costs, but only after the one I have has stopped working. I get no enjoyment out of spending money on the newest thing. Some of the shirts I have are more than ten years old, but they fit and look fine on the weekends."

"If you could imagine yourself splurging on a couple-thousand-dollar Armani suit, how would you feel?"

I laughed at this one. "I have suits that I had custom-made for me. They cost me several thousand dollars each. But I remember once I got one caught on something and I felt sick to my stomach that I had ripped it—even though I had had the suit for a few years by then. My other suits are from Brooks Brothers, which aren't cheap by most people's standards, but I don't worry as much if they get ripped or torn or my children spill something on them."

Telling him this story reminded me of how Papa put away new shirts we got him for years before wearing them. "I have this pair of Ferragamo shoes that I bought in Boston. They're the most uncomfortable shoes in the world. They look great. But they give me a blister every time I wear them, and they make my arches ache. I can't get rid of them because they cost four hundred dollars."

It wasn't lost on me, saying this out loud, that I was confusing sunk costs and opportunity costs—the opportunity cost being greater comfort in another pair of shoes.

"Where does that come from?"

"My grandfather."

"And he was the model of financial responsibility?"

"Financial responsibility and stability. He could always pay the bills, and he had enough money to buy whatever he wanted. That was wealth to me."

"And he was generous?"

"Yes. He was helpful."

"He had some of that hoarding mentality from the Great Depression, and he passed some of that anxiety on to you," Klontz said. "People who grow up in restrictive models of money, it's very hard to change. If everyone has one mind-set around money, it's harder to change. If you can point to different role models in your life who did it differently as you were growing up, it's easier to switch." I thought of my uncle—my grandfather's son—who had parlayed a football scholarship to Yale into a solid career working in investments for insurance companies in Hartford, a home in the suburbs, another on a lake in Rhode Island, and two children who were quite bright. When I was growing up, he had been a model of someone who had escaped his modest upbringing.

"What I heard from you was you saying that early on in your life you heard, 'Money is bad. It's a source of conflict,'" Klontz said. "But you also heard that you needed to be vigilant around it and to pay attention to it. You were obsessively vigilant internally, but you didn't want to have a conversation around money when it came to work. But as you moved through life, you had disconfirming evidence and you were able to switch. Some people can't do that."

He was right. And I was relieved. I had been able to take in contradictory information and apply it.

For another thirty minutes, we talked about the minutiae of the choices I had made with my personal finances, about how my wife and I saved, spent, and gave away our money, and how we thought about raising our kids so they would understand money. At that point I was exhausted from so much honest talk.

Klontz summarized what I had told him: "You came from a very tumultuous environment around money, where your mother was looking to your father for what he could provide, and he wasn't able to provide at the level she wanted. You saw that fracture. As a kid you walked away with the message that money is bad, that it's a source of intense conflict and anxiety. Your mom was anxious around money. Every now and then Grandpa would come in and save the day. You also saw that and thought, 'What is it about him that he has a set of skills around money that is very attractive?' As you're trying to deal with all that growing up, you avoided any source of conflict around money, and you were even willing to take pay for less than what you were worth because you didn't want to argue about it. At the same time, you're in a financial system that was similar to his in that you were extremely vigilant. Yet you were running into areas where it wasn't working for you. You wanted to get paid more. You were able to break through that, and through the course of time you've gone into a totally different financial comfort zone. You're in a totally different socioeconomic level and doing better and better at adjusting to it. Your comfort level around spending has steadily increased based on what you can afford, but it's also been a challenge to shake some of that out. That anxiety was highly functional, too. Being vigilant and anxious around money is highly effective. You're wanting to let go of the compulsive need to save, save, save, at the expense of enjoying what you have."

He was spot-on. But what should I do?

"You're in a good place around money," he said. "The danger zones for you are somehow limiting your willingness to appreciate what you have because something comes in and says that's extravagant. It may not be extravagant at your socioeconomic level. It may be totally appropriate. That's the part in you that you cannot necessarily trust, the part that says this is extravagant. You need to challenge it and do the math, because the math does not lie on what you can afford."

Klontz came back to the tape measure. "The other risk factors would be that you would be sacrificing everything for that security. You're not doing that, but that's the risk. You've seen and felt firsthand what it's like not to have enough. It's a pretty traumatic experience. It's a scary thing. You look at Maslow's hierarchy of needs, and if you don't have safety, security, food, what else matters? That's the risk. You're so desperately afraid of not having enough that you can't enjoy life."

I felt unburdened. Part of it was my interlocutor—I liked Klontz. But it was also being able to talk so openly with someone and to be asked the questions that would pull out and connect various strands of my money script.

"How'd I do?" I asked Britt.

"Your hand is very cold," she said.

This conversation had been even more stressful than the one from the day before, even though I had started off relaxed.

Klontz believes that conversations like ours are the future of financial planning and productive thinking about money. The emphasis would not be on returns but a discussion of what motivated people around money—how they actually thought about saving, spending, and investing. It would be more extensive than what I had gone through. One forty-five-minute session would not be enough. A strategy like this would move people to the right side of the thin green line. It would, like any effective therapy, guide people to seeing how their actions were inhibiting what they wanted to do.

How you change thinking around money and wealth is difficult and time-consuming. I don't know if I would have been open to having this discussion with a financial adviser I didn't know or someone whose qualifications I did not trust, unlike with Klontz. That feeling is common and an obvious hurdle for this type of therapy. If people aren't honest with themselves, they won't be honest with an adviser, and they won't make progress on their feelings toward money. They will continue to resist change, to their detriment.

As we walked out into the cold fall day, I thought if people could frame their thoughts on money just a little bit differently, if they could talk about spending plans instead of budgets, I think they could be happier. They would know the difference between being wealthy and rich. They could make choices to get on the right side of the thin green line, no matter how much money they had.

IT'S BETTER TO BE WEALTHY THAN RICH, EVEN IF YOU'RE POOR

I began writing this book during what I thought would be a recovery of prosperity in America. It turned out to be the start of a great and growing class divide. Occupy Wall Street and the rallying cries against the One Percent sprang up in the fall of 2011, three years after the financial crash, and disrupted the story line of the recovery. The protests made some valid points. Mostly, though, this increasing class divide, massive as it seemed, reinforced my thinking about the thin green line that divides the wealthy, in a true sense, from everyone else, rich or poor. Without an ability to predict how changes to society and government were going to impact people, more and more responsibility would fall to individuals to make the key decisions that would protect their financial futures. Knowing the difference between being wealthy and being rich is the difference between living a secure or a fraught life.

I don't doubt that income inequality exists in America today. What it means is tricky. The question I had in the back of my mind while writing this book was, what if income inequality was actually the norm and the years when that gap seemed to narrow and promise greater equality were an aberration? Then Thomas Piketty wrote *Capital in the Twenty-First Century* and confirmed my hunch. The gap between the haves and the have-nots is widening to where it was at the start of the twentieth century. But another gap was widening as well: the one between the haves and the have-mores. According to the 2013 World Wealth Report, 128,000 people— out of the more than 14 million with more than $1 million in the world—control 34.6 percent of the world's wealth. Wealthy people in London, New York, and Hong Kong have more in common with each other than they do with their countrymen. They exist together in a separate realm. At the same time, the poor are getting poorer. The US Census Bureau said in September 2011 that poverty had reached a fifty-two-year high. It also said that income levels for middle-class households had dropped back to 1997 levels. That was a good time economically, before the Internet boom and bust, the real estate boom and bust, and the terrorist attacks in New York and Washington. But for people to go back to that standard of living is not easy. Think of the Bordeaux Dilemma I discussed in chapter 3. Any such regression puts tremendous pressure on the middle class not to fall further. But if this is the new normal, knowing how to think like a wealthy person—not act like a rich person—is going to be critically important to everyone.

Unlike in past periods of wealth, the world is no longer as closed. You're not comparing yourself with your neighbors because many jobs can be sent anywhere in the world and filled easily. With that goes your financial security. It is going to be up to individuals to take responsibility for themselves, even if their neighbors appear to be enjoying themselves more, at least in the short term. Yet a minority among academics say it's hard to know what all of this worry about income inequality means, if anything. After researching the impact of income inequality on society for a decade, Harvard professor Christopher Jencks gave up on a book project. "I came to see a book with six or seven chapters that all said the same thing: it's hard to tell," he told the *New York Times*. But he added, "Something that looks bad is coming at you. Saying that we shouldn't do anything about it until we know for sure would be a bad response." Better safe than sorry is the phrase that comes to mind.

To ensure we will not be at the whim of decisions and forces we can't control, we need to change our behavior around money. Governments and corporations can offer us incentives—tax breaks or dollar-for-dollar matches in our retirement plans—but we have to be aware of them to act. People need to change how they think about their personal wealth in a way akin to vaccinations. The more of us who get vaccinated, the safer the whole population is. Likewise, the more of us who try to put our financial lives on the right side of the thin green line, the better our lives will be and the less strain there will be on the social safety net. At best I'd like people to be more aware of how their financial decisions matter, the way all smokers now know that cigarettes are bad for their health, even if they choose to continue smoking. In an ideal world, there would be consequences for behavior that ends up hurting more people than yourself—think of the health costs of smoking and the financial burden on society of spending everything and saving nothing. But I'm happy to start with some awareness around wealth and money.

The people who are truly wealthy know about the advantages and disadvantages of money and can use their wealth to create security for themselves without robbing their children of the incentives to excel. They are aware of risks and create contingency plans. They save and they live in a balanced way. What they are doing, on one level, is more basic than people believe. Mediocre Wall Street traders will always be richer than the best high school English teachers, but those teachers can be wealthier if they save more money than they need to live— something that requires the same amount of discipline that the trader would need to continue his lifestyle after he stopped working. The wealthy possess the contentment that comes from having enough, whether it is $100,000, $1 million, $100 million, or more. The rich person, whatever he or she does, is going to struggle often with balance and could end up in financial situations that force unpleasant choices.

Certainly, not everyone likes this message. When I wrote a column about my day with Tiger 21, the responses ran the gamut from support to fury. I saw these men for who they were. Despite enormous bank accounts, each one had concerns that no amount of money could fix. While I had learned something from each of them, I wasn't sure I would trade places with any of them. Though they were all wildly wealthy and successful, their lives were far more complicated than mine.

Still, after that meeting, my wife and I took action. We bought more life and disability insurance. We sold our condo in Florida for much less than we paid for it. We pared down our expenses, even though we had never spent more than we made. We didn't have any of the traditional forms of acceptable debt—credit cards, car payments, student loans. But that afternoon had lingering effects. We had a mortgage and lifestyle expenses, which we managed better. We refinanced our house to get a lower rate; we started paying down our mortgage balance more quickly. The next time we bought a car, we paid it off within a year. Those men helped to connect in my mind so many of the lessons I have gleaned from a decade of not only writing about the richest and wealthiest people in America but living among them. Selling our condo in Naples was the hardest piece of advice to follow, even though it made complete sense. Not only did we lose an enormous amount of money, we lost our place in the sun. We miss it. But it was the right thing to do: our future depends on making sound decisions, and so does everyone else's.

ACKNOWLEDGMENTS

I would like to thank my wife, Laura, for putting up with me while I wrote another book at one of the more stressful times of our lives; our daughter Virginia for making life outside of my office so much fun; and our daughter Phoebe for teaching me perspective on work and parenthood at a time when she would only sleep at night if she was in my arms.

My agent, Erika Storella, has again represented me well, and her colleagues at the Gernert Company have been there to offer counsel. Alessandra Bastagli and Dominick Anfuso acquired the idea for this book for the Free Press, and Ben Loehnen took charge of the project when the imprint was folded into Simon & Schuster. I am grateful for the first two for seeing value in the idea, but I owe an enormous debt to Ben for spending so much time on a project that wasn't his to begin with. I came to appreciate his ability to give comments with an honesty that was bracing though always helpful. I'd also like to thank Steven Boldt, the copyeditor, who gave this book a very thorough and precise read.

I would never have written about wealth had not Lionel Barber, the editor of the *Financial Times*, allowed me to create the role of wealth correspondent at the paper. Editors such as Phil Roosevelt at *Barron's*, Brian Childs at the *International Herald Tribune*, Kyle Pope at *Condé Nast Portfolio*, and Lettie Teague at *Food & Wine* allowed me to expand my knowledge. But I wouldn't have written this book if my editors and colleagues at the *New York Times* had not seen the value in a dedicated wealth columnist at a time when so much wealth disappeared in America. Tom Redburn and Kevin McKenna believed in my idea for the Wealth Matters column. Ron Lieber became a great sounding board, guide, and friend. Tara Siegel Bernard was always a happy face to see in the newsroom—and someone with whom I talked about the costs of young kids. For years Phyllis Messinger was my editor, and Jane Bornemeier has now taken over shepherding my column. Both are excellent editors, great women, and fun people to work with and talk to. Lon Teter and Tom Kuntz have been great to work with on many special sections. I'd also like to thank Cass Peterson and her copyeditors, who have saved me many times. Larry Ingrassia and Dean Murphy, as business editors, were supportive of my work.

I'd also like to thank writer friends who offered counsel on this book and more: Mark Ellwood, Urban Waite, Robert Benton, and Josh Weinstein. Alastair Reid, who was my mentor and great friend, passed away months before this book was published. He always asked about the book's progress. Money fascinated him, even though he cared so little about it nor needed any more than he had to live a truly fascinating life.

I could not have written a book like this without the openness and generosity of the people I interviewed. They took a chance in revealing so much to me. Retired admiral Ed Straw was particularly helpful in making several key introductions for me.

Lastly I'd like to thank all of the readers of my column who have e-mailed me over the years. The earnest ones with their questions and stories have provided me with ideas for many columns. But the angry ones who directed their vitriol and hatred of the rich at me were the more valuable in my seeing this book through: they convinced me that ignorance about wealth and money was so widespread and deep that this book could fill a need.

NOTES

Without always knowing it, I have been researching *The Thin Green Line* for more than a decade, since I started living among and writing about the wealthiest people in America. It began in New York City at the *Financial Times,* continued in Boston and Naples, Florida, with *Barron's,* the *International Herald Tribune, Food & Wine,* and *Condé Nast Portfolio,* and deepened in Fairfield County, Connecticut, where I moved in 2008 and began writing for the *New York Times.* This last move was perfect timing since it coincided with the collapse of the housing market and deep losses in the financial markets—two events that showed who was wealthy and who was merely rich. I cannot begin to guess how many people I have spoken to about the issues woven through this book. But generally I interview about six people a week for my column and do that fifty-two weeks a year. Multiply that by six years as of this writing for 1,872 people. That number doesn't count the people I've spoken to for other stories for the *Times,* but it's a good starting place. I mention it not to one-up other writers who often put in their notes section the number of people they have talked to for a book, but to show readers that the topic of wealth fascinates me and continues to hold my attention.

Nearly all of the people who are featured in this book I have interviewed myself. When possible, I've tried to give in the chapters themselves information to find the academic and other research. My goal has been to make it easier on a reader like me who rarely flips to this part of the book. For readers who are here, I've included the relevant citations for you.

PROLOGUE

My experience with Tiger 21 was the catalyst for this book. It took place at the group's New York headquarters on June 13, 2011. I used data from 1998 and 2006 from Paul Schervish's studies for Boston College's Center on Wealth and Philanthropy. The research can be found on its website, http://www.bc.edu/research/cwp/. I also read Dave Denison's March 9, 2008, profile of Schervish in the *New York Times Magazine.* The World Top Incomes Database is hosted on the website of the Paris School of Economics. I also read Emmanuel Saez's "Striking It Richer: The Evolution of Top Incomes in the United States," from March 2, 2012, and his paper "The Evolution of Top Incomes: A Historical and International Perspective," written with Thomas Piketty, in *American Economic Review* 96, no. 2. I found Kevin Hassett and Aparna Mathur's research in an October 24, 2012, opinion piece they wrote in the *Wall Street Journal.* I first heard of Ronald Schmidt's research in Robert Frank's *Wealth Report* blog in the *Wall Street Journal.*

CHAPTER 1

I met Richard Thaler at his home in La Jolla, California, on February 22, 2012. His book *Nudge: Improving Decisions About Health, Wealth, and Happiness,* written with Cass Sunstein, was published by Yale University Press in April 2008. He detailed his graduate school experience in *Quasi Rational Economics,* published by the Russell Sage Foundation in 1991. I gathered information on retirement savings from the Employee Benefit Research Institute, http://www.ebri.org/pdf/FF.271.ShortRet.6Mar14.pdf, as well as the Pension Benefit Guarantee Corporation, http://www.pbgc.gov/blog/post/2013/09/19/EBRI-Report-Says-Pension-Plan-Participation-Goes-Up-Contributions-Come-Down.aspx.

CHAPTER 2

I interviewed Jeannie Krieger on January 24, 2011, and some of what we talked about appeared in a February 9, 2011, story I wrote in the *New York Times.* I first met her son-in-law Joe Duran at Bouchon Bakery in the Time Warner Center on January 13, 2011, and I've interviewed him a half dozen times since then, with all of those conversations feeding into this chapter. Michael Duncan came to our house on June 19, 2012. Brad Klontz and I undertook our study of the One Percent by surveying 1,090 random participants. The study, which was published in the *Journal of Financial Planning* in December 2014, looked at the differences between the One Percent and people in the top 5 percent and the top 20 percent. We defined the One Percent as people with more than $370,000 in annual income and/or a net worth of $2.5 million. (We did not think we would get enough respondents if we limited it to the true cutoff for net worth of over $10 million.) The 5 percent earned $154,643 a year and the 20 percent earned $87,606. I interviewed Gregg S. Fisher in his office in New

York on April 12, 2012. I had spoken with him and Philip Z. Maymin about their investor study on March 8, 2011. Their study "The
Curse of Knowledge: When and Why Risk Parity Beats Tangency"
was published in the *Journal of Wealth Management* that year. I interviewed Don Phillips of Morningstar on February 20, 2013. I spoke
with Daylian Cain of Yale's School of Management on January 23,
2012, and again on December 5, 2012. I spoke with Nicholas Stuller
of AdviceIQ on June 21, 2012. I interviewed Terrance Odean on January 13, 2012. His paper "All That Glitters: The Effect of Attention
and News on the Buying Behavior of Individual and Institutional
Investors" was published in the *Review of Financial Studies* in 2008.

CHAPTER 3

Data on Darien, Connecticut, came from the 2010 US Census Bureau survey data. I met Susan Bruno on November 9, 2012. I read
about Mark Rank's research in "From Rags to Riches to Rags," which
appeared in the Sunday Review section of the *New York Times* on
April 18, 2014. I interviewed Armando Roman on January 6, 2014.
Data on consumer debt is from USA Quick Facts compiled by the
US Census Bureau. The Consumer Federation of America report
was released in February 2014. Details on Patricia Kluge's financial
problems came from the Charlottesville, Virginia, press reports at the
time.

CHAPTER 4

I attended Bradley Birkenfeld's hearing in Fort Lauderdale, Florida,
on June 19, 2008, for a story I was writing for *Condé Nast Portfolio*. I
went to Weymouth, Massachusetts, on July 24, 2008.

CHAPTER 5

I interviewed Paul Posluszny on February 25, 2011, in downtown Manhattan, when I also met with Ron Carson. I spoke with Posluszny again by phone on May 29, 2012, and talked to Carson several times in 2011 and 2012. I interviewed Adam Carriker on June 1, 2012. I spoke with Mark Curtis on February 22, 2013, with Michael Conway June 11, 2012, and with Don Ross on May 21, 2012. I met with Stuart Sternberg on May 22, 2012, at Kneaded Bread in Port Chester, New York. I met with Tim Noonan on April 1, 2014, at Rosie in New Canaan, Connecticut. I interviewed Ed Marinaro on April 20, 2012, and Roger Staubach on June 8, 2012.

CHAPTER 6

I went to the Westover School on May 10, 2012. I interviewed Susan Beacham three times, first on July 17, 2012. The paper "Rich Dad, Smart Dad: Decomposing the Intergenerational Transmission of Income" appeared in the *Journal of Political Economy* in April 2012. I first talked to Shamus Khan on August 26, 2010, and met him at a Columbia University conference on inequality on October 5, 2010. I spoke to him again in 2012 and 2013. His book *Privilege: The Making of an Adolescent Elite at St. Paul's School* was published by Princeton University Press in 2010. Sean F. Reardon's research appeared in *Whither Opportunity?: Rising Inequality, Schools, and Children's Life Chances*, published by the Russell Sage Foundation in 2011. I sat with James Heckman at the University of Chicago's Harris School of Public Policy on February 17, 2012, and spoke with him subsequently by phone. The then-unpublished paper I referenced was "Hard Evidence on Soft Skills," written with Tim Kautz. I also referred to another paper, "The Rate of Return to the High/Scope Perry Preschool Program," published in 2009 in the NBER Working Papers series. The North Carolina study can be found at http://nyti.ms/1pdjEEq.

CHAPTER 7

I met James Grubman in New York on March 13, 2014. Randi Kreger's research appeared as "What Have You Done for Me Lately? Entitlement: A Key Narcissistic Trait" on a *Psychology Today* blog in October 2011. I met Randy Fertel on March 29, 2012, at Domenica in New Orleans. His book, *The Gorilla Man and the Empress of Steak*, was published by University Press of Mississippi in 2011. I spoke with Naomi Sobel on July 12 and 17, 2012. Barry Schwartz's *The Paradox of Choice: Why More Is Less* was published in 2004 by Ecco. I spoke to Roy Williams on July 17, 2012. His book *Preparing Heirs: Five Steps to a Successful Transition of Family Wealth and Values*, with Vic Preisser, was published in 2010 by Robert Reed Publishers. Jay Zagorsky's "Do People Save or Spend Their Inheritances? Understanding What Happens to Inherited Wealth" was published in the *Journal of Family Economic Issues* in 2012. I spoke to Franco Lombardo on July 13, 2012. I spoke to Doug Ideker and his adviser Jeff Ladouceur on July 12, 2012.

CHAPTER 8

I first interviewed Barbara and Donald Jonas in early 2006. I have followed up on their foundation's progress every two years since then. The full finding from the Jonas study on nursing impact is "A full-time nursing educator in a baccalaureate program may teach roughly 300 students per year, assuming three classes of 50 students each per semester, and two semesters per year. Over the course of a 25-year career, that educator will prepare 7,500 nurses. An average RN might care for ten different patients over a four-day workweek, 48 weeks per year. Over a 30-year career, that nurse will care for 14,400 patients. Thus, the 7,500 nurses trained by one faculty member collectively touch the lives of 3.6 million patients a year over the course of a 30-year career." The Credit Suisse survey was released in conjunction with the Forbes 400 Summit on Philanthropy in September 2012. I spoke to Pierre Omidyar on November 15, 2012. I spoke with Paul Piff on January 21, 2013. Papers of his that I have drawn on include "My Brother's Keeper? Compassion Predicts Generosity More Among Less Religious Individuals," *Journal of Social Psychological and Personality Science,* 2012; "For Whom Do the Ends Justify the Means? Social Class and Utilitarian Moral Judgment," *Journal of Personality and Social Psychology,* 2012; "Having Less, Giving More: The Influence of Social Class on Prosocial Behavior," *Journal of Personality and Social Psychology,* 2010; and "Class, Chaos, and the Construction of Community," *Journal of Personality and Social Psychology,* 2012. I interviewed Charles Bronfman on November 9, 2009, and September 14, 2012, around the publication of his two books, *The Art of Giving* and *The Art of Doing Good,* both published by Jossey-Bass. I interviewed Jon Huntsman Sr. on October 29, 2013. Arthur Brooks, president of the American Enterprise Institute, talked about his philosophy on giving at Brigham Young University on February 24, 2009.

CHAPTER 9

I traveled to Manhattan, Kansas, on November 28–30, 2012. The Klontz studies I referred to are "Money Beliefs and Financial Behaviors: Development of the Klontz Money Script Inventory," *Journal of Financial Therapy,* 2011; and "Disordered Money Behaviors: Development of the Klontz Money Behavior Inventory," *Journal of Financial Therapy,* 2012.

EPILOGUE

I read about Christopher Jencks's research in Eduardo Porter's column "Income Equality: A Search for Consequences" in the *New York Times,* March 25, 2014.

INDEX